THE GROWTH OF THE
WORK/LIFE
movement
IN CORPORATE AMERICA

THE GROWTH OF THE
WORK/LIFE
movement
IN CORPORATE AMERICA

AND THE PROFESSIONALS
WHO MADE IT HAPPEN

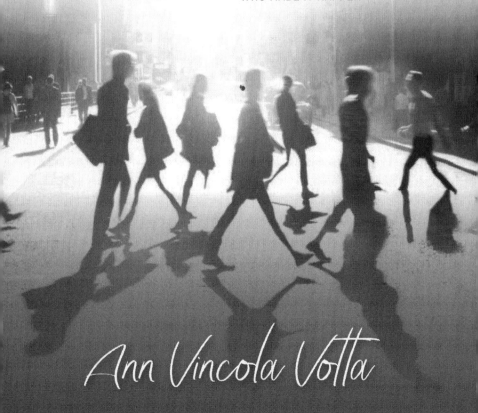

Ann Vincola Votta

The Growth of the Work/Life Movement in Corporate America . . . and the
Professionals Who Made It Happen

For information about this title or to order other books and/or electronic media,
contact the publisher:

AV Publishing LLC
1176 Tahiti Parkway
Sarasota, FL 34236
AV Publishers.com
508-221-8650

Library of Congress Control Number: 2023914483

ISBNs:
978-0-9889757-7-4 (softcover)
978-0-9889757-8-1 (eBook)

Printed in the United States of America

Cover and Interior design: 1106 Design

Publisher's Cataloging-in-Publication Data
Names: Votta, Ann Vincola, 1943- .
Title: The growth of the work/life movement in corporate America : and the pro-
    fessionals who made it happen / Ann Vincola Votta.
Description: Sarasota, FL : AV Publishing, LLC, 2023. | Includes bibliographic
    references.
Identifiers: LCCN: 2023914483 | ISBN 9780988975774 (pbk.) | ISBN
    9780988975781 (ebook)
Subjects: LCSH: Work-life balance. | Work and family. | Job satisfaction. |
    Personnel management—United States—History. | BISAC: BUSINESS &
    ECONOMICS / Workplace Culture. | BUSINESS & ECONOMICS /
    Human Resources & Personnel Management. | BUSINESS &
    ECONOMICS / Corporate & Business History.
Classification: LCC HD6955.V68 2023 | DDC 658.3 V--dc23
LC record available at https://lccn.loc.gov/2023914483

DEDICATION

To all my brilliant friends and colleagues, who became the pioneers
of the work/life field and began working diligently forty years ago
to raise CEO awareness to promote the concept
that work/life balance matters.

Also by Ann Vincola Votta

Reunited: When the Past Becomes a Present

From Italy and Back: Coming Full Circle

Acknowledgments

I spent twenty years of my professional life working alongside of (and oftentimes competing against) some outstanding and dedicated individuals—many of whom became very good friends of mine. We achieved remarkable success raising awareness on the part of corporate executives to prove that the development of work and family, or work/life benefits, could influence their bottom line in a positive way. We were driven.

With that said, it is my number one aim to acknowledge the work undertaken by all of these individuals and organizations, as we worked vigorously and continued on the journey. I have tried to include as many names as my brain and memory allows, but I am sure that I may have missed a few. That is not intentional. Many professionals from various disciplines entered the picture over two decades, which essentially created our movement. We were considered *Pioneers*, and rightfully so. Many of us became nationally recognized for our efforts. We advocated for groundbreaking change, by making the business case for the value of adding a work and family agenda to employee benefits packages.

It is hard to believe that these efforts began over forty years ago. My focus in this book is to concentrate on the decades between 1981 to 2001—the twenty years of my involvement in the arena. I readily admit, that during the most recent twenty-plus years, I have had little to do with the field and its continued growth and advancement, although I have been peripherally involved with the activity within the domain by staying informed through LinkedIn and other social media outlets about corporate attention to work/life balance.

When my colleagues and I started on this journey the internet was just becoming mainstream, and we had nowhere near the resources available to us that are so readily accessed today. Most of what is to follow is how I remember it, including the chronology of events and the professionals involved. However, I have taken the liberty of reviewing some events, statistics, articles, and career paths through Google and Wikipedia to enhance and substantiate my memory. Sometimes I may veer back and forth in time as I tell my story, and my timeline may appear disjointed. I do not wish to confuse my reader; I only wish to focus on the highlights as I experienced them and to relay their importance in my personal journey.

I have not included the names of the many extraordinary corporate CEOs and human resource executives who made an impact on the movement by being forward-thinking enough to take a chance and add work/life programs to their company's employee benefits package. Nevertheless, we owe them a debt of gratitude for the part they played in the creation of our movement by speaking at our conferences and helping us to drive the agenda forward. Without them, there never would have been a movement. They were remarkable individuals who took giant risks by changing corporate culture within their organizations.

It is also not my purpose here to delve into how work/life has evolved today in the corporate arena, nor to describe the programs which are so much a part of the current corporate/institutional scene. I am not focusing on how work/life balance is perceived today, nor what it might look like in the future. I leave that to the myriad of professionals in the human resource arena working very hard to tackle those issues. I do believe, however, that we established a foundation for the future, and that is why I have detailed the types of programs that flourished during our time.

Special thanks go to those individuals I feel influenced me the most, and to those who kept pushing us forward, particularly the friends with whom I worked to create The National Work Family Alliance and AWLP (The Alliance of Work/Life Professionals). Essentially, the development of those two groups and the conferences our organizations presented, are what I am most proud. Those individuals know who they are.

I would like to thank the colleagues with whom I spoke as I started on this journey. They helped jog my memory and kept me on track—and offered encouragement. Mary Ellen Gornick, Cathy Leibow, Pam Kerns, Kathy Cramer, Joan Heminway, Clark Adams, and Paul Neveu, all added bits of information that were invaluable to me. Dr. Desiree DelZio, a new addition to the current field, read my manuscript and provided me with insights that I never would have been able to understand without her input. And my daughter, Leigh Vincola, my forever editor and writing guru, as usual provided guidance in structure, balance, and tone. And, of course, thanks go to my husband, Alan Votta, who always offers his support and encouragement, in everything I do, particularly in my writing endeavors.

I have authored two other books—both personal memoirs. I consider this book a memoir as well. I would like to call it a professional memoir, since it is my recollection of events, people, organizations, businesses, and institutions that played a major role in creating a new field that started a movement. I am grateful to have taken part in it.

This is my story about a moment in time, or twenty years within history—about how the work/life movement impacted my life, and how I impacted it.

Contents

CONTENTS

Introduction

As I enter my ninth decade on this planet, I am reminded every day of a time in my professional life that was vibrant, exciting, and important—important to me and to my many friends and colleagues who played an integral part in it. The 'it' was the creation and development of the work/life movement in the U.S.

That is not to say that it was always smooth sailing. It was usually a struggle—an uphill battle, if you will. I am reminded of the myth of Sisyphus, i.e., rolling the rock to the top of the mountain only to have it fall back again. We were constantly faced with the arduous task of making the business case for instituting new programs within the workplace. Sometimes it felt that small steps forward weren't enough for the huge culture change we were working toward, and we somehow would slip back again.

We needed the support and backing of corporate executives, and we needed one another. Many new businesses started during this time—their main purpose being to offer direct services or consulting help in order to achieve our goals. Although we got along, it was a competitive environment—one in which some made considerable personal financial gain. And we formed alliances; although, frankly, in the beginning several key leaders in the field were not inclined to collaborate, as some of us began to coalesce and join forces.

Only a few of the companies/service providers that came onto the scene in the early to mid-80s, still exist today. Those companies have necessarily changed, modified, and expanded their scope and services or merged with other larger companies in order to meet the newer demands of a changing workplace and workforce. Today the emphasis is more on mental health and well-being for everyone, rather than on dependent care services. I will discuss those services and service providers later.

In fact, as I proceeded on this reflective journey, I was reminded of some not-so-pleasant memories of failed partnerships and considerable backstabbing that was undeniably part of that competitive environment. I was more of a negotiator, and my successes came with attempting to bring people together, rather than exemplifying a killer-like business acumen. I gave away more consulting hours than I'd care to admit during my years within the field!

My professional career changed over time—from educator to consultant to retail business owner to writer; however, the period between 1981 to 2001 became, for me, the most intense and engaged stretch of time I experienced. I was in on the beginning of the development of the work/life movement and, I and my colleagues, played a major role in making it happen. We were pioneers—trailblazers—innovators!

During the 80s and 90s, real change took place in the expansion of awareness—awareness on the part of corporate executives that the development of employee benefit programs could have a positive impact on the work/life balance needs of their employees, and consequently, on their bottom line, too. The transformation actually started during the 70s when women entered the workforce in huge numbers.

The effect of the women's liberation movement changed a woman's role from that of stay-at-home mother to working woman, and therefore, as we reached the 80s, the need for child care was a growing concern in the country. Attention to how work and family intersected and how a balance could be achieved for individuals became a major goal for human resource professionals throughout corporate America. In fact, the terminology initially was work/family rather than work/life, and the emphasis was clearly on dependent care.

And, understandably, most of us who started this movement came from the child care arena, i.e., early childhood education and social work. We were so aware of the need for quality and affordable care, not only because it was part of our jobs, but because we were women—and we were mothers! We were living it—as well as describing it. Of course, there were men in the new field, too, although they were definitely in the minority. We were most grateful to have those very special men among us working for our combined goals. They understood the struggle and they helped to make a difference, and they became a very integral part of our growing movement.

What is work/life balance? When I began this journey of looking back and writing down my thoughts, I searched on Amazon to see how many books included the term "work/life balance" in the title. At first glance, I found over one hundred and fifty titles listed. The books are mostly about how to achieve a personal work/life balance for individuals, rather than looking at the industry in general, but I was amazed at how the term has expanded in breadth and scale since I was intimately involved in the field. There is even a work/life balance site on LinkedIn that very actively promotes the concept to help individuals achieve a balance in their lives.

There are many definitions for work/life balance cited in journals and articles, but to me, the best way to describe work/life balance is that it is "a healthy balance between an individual's work responsibilities and the demands of one's personal and family needs."

In today's post-covid world, everyone is concerned with balance and how best to live an integrated life. Work-at-home and working remotely have become the norm, rather than an unusual benefit, and zooming during the covid years gave individuals, as well as companies, a new way to communicate, which has, in some cases, kept some employees continuing to work remotely. Today people are more obsessed with making time for oneself in order to avoid burnout and to be most efficient and comfortable in personal life choices. Attention to the availability of the programs that we worked so hard to institute has never been more necessary than they are today. That is why programs that provide more flexibility to employees, like job-sharing, hybrid schedules, or sabbaticals (including work-at-home) help to retain the best and brightest in any workforce.

What ultimately emerged as the work/life movement came from an initial emphasis on the intersection of work and the family, because of the very real need for child care services for the working woman, regardless of whether that entry into the workforce was to enhance one's career or for financial need. Through the years the development of child care programs expanded, and the field grew to encompass elder care programs, flexible work policies, human resources, employee benefits, employee assistance programs (EAPs), corporate culture change, diversity, organizational effectiveness, recruitment and retention, and much more.

Likewise, my career within the field changed and evolved too. I was a child care specialist to begin with and by the time I left the industry, I was nationally recognized as a human resource and benefits expert, albeit with an emphasis on dependent care. Today the priority has switched to be more inclusive of the individual, applying the label DEI—Diversity, Equity, Inclusion. Professionals in the field are now concentrating their efforts on how unique and diverse individuals can function effectively in the workplace, while having their work and personal life demands met. I see that as more of a recognition placed on the individual within society, rather than on the family generally, embracing all differences and lifestyles. I think most would agree that the two strands—work/life balance and DEI should be aligned and complementary in any corporate HR strategy.

This book has been brewing in my mind for a very long time, and I have finally determined that I must put pen to paper (or fingers on the computer) to look back and remember how it all started and to recognize the small part I played in making it happen. But more importantly, to acknowledge the passion and devotion that several key people brought to the table to make a difference.

While undertaking this journey of looking back, I was able to retrieve many of the articles authored by me that were published in HR publications, particularly in the final years of my participation in the work/life world. I was recognized as an expert in the field by that time, and my opinion was often sought. It is gratifying to learn that I have still been quoted in scholarly journals and other works so many years later.

I like to network and I pride myself on the ability to bring people together. During the 80s and 90s, several of my colleagues and friends began talking and meeting and ultimately formed alliances and organizations that had a huge impact on the growing field. That is how we got the ball rolling. And, incidentally, all of that involvement was on a volunteer basis. In fact, several get-to-gethers took place at my vacation home on Martha's Vineyard. Those meetings cemented relationships and became the foundation for several organizations that followed, i.e. The Association of Child Care Consultants International (ACCI) and The National Work Family Alliance, which emerged to become The Alliance for Work/Life Professionals (AWLP). It was a head-y time for us.

Special friends at my home on Martha's Vineyard, 1999.
Carey Fleming, Ann Vincola, Madeline Fried, Pam Kerns.

HISTORY AND BACKGROUND

1

How It All Began

The Economy and HR Benefits

When the economy is good, U.S. corporate CEOs will continuously look for ways to enhance their bottom line, to retain the best and the brightest workers, and to increase productivity. I maintain that in the early 80s when the work/life movement got its start, the need was for more employer-supported child care to assist working women as they entered the workforce in huge numbers—thus the investigation into how the development of an on-site center (or a resource and referral system to aid in finding suitable and affordable child care) could have a direct effect on a company's growth and profitability. Those services were the most sought after to begin with. And that is how I got started within the field, i.e., by providing consulting services to help companies consider on-site child care.

We began by conducting needs assessments to convince corporate executives that there was a direct cost/benefit to creating those types of programs, particularly providing an on-site child care facility. By designing a survey that was specific to each company and conducting focus groups with employees, we could determine whether providing that unique employee benefit would indeed be beneficial to the entire company.

The U. S. economy in the 1970s suffered from rising inflation and *stagflation*, which continued into the early 1980s, causing severe economic recession until 1982. But by 1983, the economy rebounded and enjoyed a sustained period of growth for the remainder of the 80s and part of the 1990s. All of that impacted productivity and increased awareness on the part of CEOs to do all that they could to enhance recruitment and retention at their workplace.

Thus, the economic climate by 1983 was such that it enabled those of us, who were espousing increased employee benefits, to be successful in convincing corporate execs, particularly human resource executives, that providing dependent care services made sense.

As the economy started improving in the country, after the inflation and recession of the 70s, several new programs and businesses began to pop up and attention became focused on the provision of employer-supported child care.

Early Activity and Programs Within the New Field

In 1981 I was Assistant Professor of Early Childhood Education at Stonehill College in North Easton, Massachusetts, when I became fascinated with the concept of employer-supported child care. As I began investigating employer-supported child care and understood that there was a lack of good quality and affordable care, especially in remote areas, I became aware of what others were doing in the field as well. That investigation encouraged me to become more immersed in what ultimately grew into the work/life movement. The people and groups that I mention in the following paragraphs are the ones that influenced me the most and had a direct bearing on the industry.

One of the most influential pioneers in the field was Dana Friedman. In 1980/81 Dana was completing her doctoral program at Harvard Business School and sought input for her dissertation on the development of employer-supported child care. I contacted Dana after she published a survey in a local newspaper, seeking more statistics to prove that the lack of quality child care was a problem for working parents. Dana continued her work first at *The Conference Board* and then when she and Ellen Galinsky founded *The Families and Work Institute* in New York City. Dana remained a giant within the field, and I very much valued her work.

Gwen Morgan, the doyenne of the child care world in the very early days, served as a professor within a new master's degree program at Lesley University in Cambridge, Massachusetts—a program which later set the stage for campus on-site child care. I enrolled in that master's program at Lesley. The curriculum included a groundbreaking course, taught by Gwen, on day care licensing. Earlier (1972), Gwen was named the first Director of the Massachusetts Office for Children (at a salary of a dollar a year, by the way), a newly formed agency that dealt with everything related to child care in the state. Massachusetts had some of the most stringent child care licensing requirements, which proved to be a very solid grounding to assess a good quality child care environment. People do not realize that Gwen Morgan's contribution to the work/life field is enormous. I believe that she was the one who truly got everything started. Gwen passed away in 2015. She is sorely missed, but her legacy lives on.

Gwen Morgan eventually moved from teaching at Lesley University in Cambridge, Massachusetts, to Wheelock College in Boston, Massachusetts. Wheelock became the first home of *Work/Family Directions*—a nationwide resource and referral network to help parents locate child care for their children. Gwen and Francene Sussner Rodgers were the co-founders of the service, established initially to provide resource and referral services to IBM employees, their first very significant client. IBM approached Gwen with their child care dilemma, i.e., helping their employees find suitable care. Work/Family Directions became the first major provider of dependent care resource and referral services for corporate clients. WFD, as it was later called, evolved to become the premier consulting organization in work/life and, only recently, closed. Fran Rodgers continued to be a driving force in the newly created field and a major influencer for all of us, as she led Work/Family Directions to forge and shape new paths.

I met with both Fran and Gwen as I was embarking on my new endeavor, i.e., creating my own company, *Corporate Child Care Consultants*. Gwen encouraged me to join WFD, rather than start my own thing. And Fran wasn't all that pleased that I was entering the fray, as I sat in her kitchen while she fed her infant daughter in her highchair, and we discussed the new emerging field. I did not follow Gwen's advice, nor did I worry about Fran's displeasure at my becoming a competitor!

Two other companies providing resource and referral services to corporate clients joined the field in those early days. They were *The Partnership Group* owned by Tyler Phillips, and

Dependent Care Consultants started by John Place. The Partnership Group was later purchased by Ceridian, and Dependent Care Consultants evolved to become *LifeCare* with Peter Burki at the helm, and still operates today.

In 1982 at the NAEYC (National Association for the Education of Young Children) annual conference, I was delighted to meet with Sandy Burud, who ultimately became my partner several years later when we formed Summa Associates, and we discussed her recently published book, *Employer-Supported Child Care: Investing in Human Resources.* Her research in that study provided the ammunition we all needed to see the increase in employer-supported child care become a reality for many companies. Sandy was instrumental in opening an on-site child care center for Union Bank at their headquarters in Santa Monica, California, which became a model for corporate on-site centers.

At that conference I also met Karen Woodford and Nadine Mathis from Tempe, Arizona, consulting partners who had recently helped develop a corporate on-site center for America West Airlines in Phoenix, Arizona. Karen and Nadine also eventually became my partners in Summa Associates. (More on Summa Associates later.)

I was also aware of the work that both Susan Ginsberg and Ellen Galinsky, instructors at Bank Street College in New York City at the time, were doing with campus child care. Eventually, Ellen Galinsky and Dana Friedman formed *The Families and Work Institute* in New York City, an organization that had a huge impact on the burgeoning field and became a major player, not only in promoting the concept of work and family, but also in relation to research projects, especially Ellen Galinsky's contribution of continuing research on the brain and child development.

Ellen Galinsky also served as President of NAEYC for a few years, and she still plays an enormous role in advocacy for child care on the national scene. She was recently elected President of the Work and Family Researchers Network. Arlene Johnson joined the two founders at Families and Work Institute a few years later, and likewise became a recognized expert in the field. Susan Ginsberg was a founder and member of our AWLP Board, and for years published the *Work and Family Life Newsletter*, which became the premier resource for information on child care for working parents. Sadly, Susan passed away in 2018. She was a dear friend and I miss her.

Roger Brown and his wife Linda Mason were beginning to investigate the child care arena prior to establishing their company—Bright Horizons Children's Centers, the current premier provider of quality on-site child care, after they merged with Corporate Family Solutions to operate as Bright Horizons Family Solutions. Linda and Roger had recently returned from Africa after having worked for *Save the Children*, and they knew little about operating day care centers, and they needed to be educated. In fact, they sat in my living room in Brookline, Massachusetts, to pick my brain and learn what they could about child care in general. I was very accommodating! As they got their start, they became my primary competitor in going after corporate clients, until I changed my consulting emphasis to focus more on flexible work policies, rather than exclusively on on-site care.

Faith Wohl was another luminary within our field as it began to take shape. Following the death of her beloved husband, Faith went to work at Dupont in 1973. She held various leadership positions in public relations, corporate communications, and human resources over the twenty years she spent at Dupont. She made a name for herself focusing on issues related to women in the workplace, and she helped change workplace culture at Dupont. She then held several political appointments during the Clinton Administrations and continued to advocate for family friendly policies. In 1997 she became President of the Child Care Action Campaign, a national nonprofit advocacy organization based in New York City that worked to strengthen families, improve education, and advance the well-being of children with good quality, safe, affordable child care. I first met Faith in 1975 when she did a staff training for my staff when I was Director of the Simmons College Child Care Center. She was an enormous inspiration to me, and I fondly recall our many interactions. I was saddened to learn of her passing in 2022 at the age of eight-five.

Roger Neugebauer began publishing *Exchange Magazine*, a resource for professional development for all early childhood providers. Roger and I met back in 1972. He was in the same master's program as me at Lesley University, and he was prompted by none other than Gwen Morgan to start the magazine, because she saw that there was a crying need for such a publication for child care workers. Roger and his wife, Bonnie, remain co-owners of the magazine, which is still published today. Roger and Bonnie then went on to found *The World Forum Foundation*, which presented *The World Forum on Early Care Conferences* around the globe. I was lucky enough to participate in one of his early conferences that was held in Singapore in 2000. I was privileged to serve as a seminar leader in one of the workshops.

As I mentioned earlier, Boston was way ahead of the game when it came to providing quality care, whether it be corporate, institutional, or campus care. Two important centers in the Boston area stood out at the time when I was beginning to become involved. One was the on-site child care center at The Stride Rite Corporation in Cambridge, Massachusetts. CEO Arnold Hiatt became an early spokesperson for on-site care and encouraged fellow corporate execs who might have needed a little push. Karen Liebold was the center director, and she became a good friend to the New England ESCCN (Employer-Supported Child Care Network.)

I also became friendly with Sue Halloran, who was the director of the *Government Center Child Care Center* located at the Transportation Building in Boston. That center was one of the first government run facilities and it led the way for other institutional facilities to provide on-site care. Sue served on the Board of the ESCCN with me.

West Coast child care providers were also entering the picture as we approached the 90s—Judy David, the Director of One Small Step, The Bay Area Employer Work & Family Association in San Francisco; and Kathy Tama, who helped open an on-site child care center at Pacific Gas and Electric, and then went on to serve as a consultant within the new work/life industry. Cathy Leibow rose to manager level at Intel, but left the company after the search for child care for her special needs child became impossible, and she started her own company, *FamilyCare, Inc.* Cathy has continued in the industry concentrating on concierge services and recently joined *Circles North America* as Vice President of Business Development.

Another notable West Coast luminary is Ken Dychtwald, the Founder and CEO of Age Wave. Ken is a psychologist and gerontologist and has been recognized as the foremost visionary on everything relating to aging and the elderly. I met Ken at a seminar he presented for us at the Getty Museum in Los Angeles, California, when I was at Work/Life Benefits. His attention to our aging population has been enormous and its impact has been monumental.

In those early days, several other child care and early care experts entered the scene by establishing their own consulting firms—Madeline Fried of *Fried and Sher* in Virginia, Mary Ellen Gornick of *The CPA Group* in Chicago, Mary Brown and Betsy Richards of *BrownRichards and Associates* in Atlanta, and me, Ann Vincola of *Corporate Child Care Consultants* in Boston.

As you can clearly see, there was a good deal going on and interest was mounting exponentially on the concept of offering working parents more assistance in securing good quality care for their children in the corporate arena, on college campuses, and at other institutions across the nation. I have highlighted the aforementioned players because I was personally connected with each of them very early on in the development of the work/life movement and in my journey within the field.

The Pioneers

Clark Adams

Barbara Adolf

Mary Brown

Roger Brown

Sandy Burud

Kathy Cramer

Judy David

Donna Dolan

Stephanie Fanjul

Carey Fleming

Madeleine Fried

Dana Friedman

Ellen Galinsky

Dave Gleason

Bradley Googins

Mary Ellen Gornick

Susan Ginsberg

Sue Halloran

Arlene Johnson

Pam Kerns

Stanley Kuziel

Cathy Leibow

Nadine Mathis

Gwen Morgan

Roger Neugebauer

Tyler Phillips

Betsy Richards

Fran Sussner Rodgers

Karol Rose

Susan Seitel

Kathy Tama

Ann Vincola

Faith Wohl

Karen Woodford

[*Note:* The Pioneers listed are individuals who started in the field in the early 80s and with whom I had a direct connection.]

2

Work/Life Programs and Services

Before detailing my involvement and journey into the work/life field, I want to describe the many new programs and services that became a vital part of the movement. Thank goodness there were knowledgeable entrepreneurs who saw a need and a void and capitalized on it.

As mentioned earlier, the emphasis was clearly on dependent care and the need for child care services was the impetus that started the ball rolling. However, it became clear that there was a need for elder care services as well. Many working parents soon were labeled as "the Sandwich Generation" i.e., those people caught in-between the two—needing both child care and elder care services. Many people had no idea whatsoever how to look for or how to procure elder care services. On-site child care centers and resource and referral programs helped identify dependent care services that employees desperately needed.

- On-or-Near-Site Child Care Centers

Most companies initially got involved in providing work/life programs when they began investigating the viability of providing an on-or-near site child care facility. It was an expensive proposition, but CEOs soon realized that there could be a return on their investment in recruitment and retention of employees. Child care experts were hired as consultants to assist in the decision-making and in the design and development of the center. Many of those early centers operated as a division within the company, but later were outsourced to for-profit providers.

- Resource and Referral Services

Employees needed help in finding care for their children and care for the elders in their lives. Several major players became the companies that provided that service to their corporate clients, including Work/Family Directions, The Partnership Group, and Dependent Care Consultants/Life Care. Many local resource and referral agencies and smaller companies sprang up as well. Therefore, resource and referral became the number one service throughout the industry. These services enabled parents to find suitable, affordable, quality care for their children and for the elders in their care.

- Flexible Work Policies

As the field developed it became apparent that there was also a need for more flexibility within every workforce. Every needs assessment performed at any given company always pointed to employee desire for flexibility, therefore, programs like job-sharing, work-at-home, reduced hours, and sabbaticals became the new nomenclature. And those of us who were the professionals in the new field became expert in describing the new concepts and promoting them.

- Work/Life as Part of an Employee Benefits Package

As dependent care, resource and referral, and flexible work policies became increasingly available, these services were seen as part of the total employee benefits package, and many forward-thinking employers were influential in seeing that the services became part of the larger package. *SHRM, the Society for Human Resource Management*, helped in achieving that goal, by highlighting these programs and giving them the attention they deserved.

- Integration of Wellness and Employee Assistance Programs (EAPs)

As we proceeded down the path of making work/life part of the corporate scene, we became more knowledgeable about the intersection of Wellness and Employee Assistance Programs (EAPs). It made sense to integrate them wherever possible. Wellness programs added attention to healthy lifestyles, weight loss programs, smoking cessation workshops, for example, and EAP programs provided a focus on mental health issues, and alcohol and substance abuse programs. These programs have expanded their scope over the years, and have become very necessary to a complete package of employee benefits.

- Maternity and Paternity Leave

The Family and Medical Leave Act of 1993 entitled eligible employees to take unpaid leave for specified family and medical reasons with a continuation of group health insurance coverage. The act enabled parents, both new and adoptive mothers and fathers, to take up to twelve weeks leave. It was groundbreaking legislation that furthered the cause and helped all working parents. Generous maternity and paternity leave policies continue to be an important perk that employees seek when accepting a new job.

- Diversity Workshops

As awareness grew and workforces became more diverse, it became apparent that there was a need for training on how to deal with differences. Sexual harassment workshops and diversity workshops became an integral part of HR training programs. These workshops essentially became the forerunner of the focus of diversity, equity and inclusion programs (DEI), so prevalent in the workplace today.

One of the most important individuals in the field of diversity was Dr. Roosevelt Thomas Jr. As the CEO of his own consulting organization, he was a cultural diversity pioneer and was at the forefront of developing a framework for diversity management in corporations. He was a consultant to many Fortune 500 companies, government entities, non-profit organizations and academic institutions. I was fortunate enough to have met Dr. Thomas and presented with him on several occasions. I am grateful for all that he taught me. Dr. Thomas passed away in 2013.

- Back-Up Child Care

More and more companies opened their own on-site child care centers; however, it soon became apparent that there was also a need for care when regular child care arrangements broke down; for example, when an in-home provider or day care home provider was ill. Back-Up Child Care Centers became the answer. Several companies provided only back-up care either on-site or near-site.

- Concierge Services

As workforces grew and became more diverse, employees who were not parents also demanded attention. Thus, services like travel planning, dinner reservations, meal planning, dry cleaning pick-up, dog watching, etc. were included under the term 'concierge services.' Equity for all employees was the name of the game. Expanded concierge services are very much a part of today's corporate scene.

It is clearly evident that as time went on and awareness grew, new and innovative programs were initiated, and professionals continued to provide those services in order to fill the need.

The Major Players

Work/Family Directions

Families and Work Institute

The Partnership Group

Bright Horizons

Corporate Family Solutions

Boston College Center for Work and Family

DCC—Dependent Care Consultants/LifeCare

Corporate Child Care Consultants

Workplace Options

Brown Richards

Summa Associates

Fried and Sher

Workplace Solutions

Catalyst

The Conference Board

Work and Family Life Newsletter

The CPA Group

ACCCI

WFC Resources

Child Care Action Campaign (CCAC)

One Small Step

MY JOURNEY

3

Contracts and Projects

From 1979 to 1982 I was a Professor of Early Childhood
Education at Stonehill College in North Easton, Massachusetts.
For many years, I had attended and presented at the annual conference of The National Association for the Education of Young
Children (NAEYC). Attending the conference in 1982 changed
me and my career direction. I met other child care professionals
who were beginning to talk about employer-supported child care
and a spark was ignited in me, so much so, that by the end of
the academic year, I left my job at Stonehill and started my own
consulting firm—*Corporate Child Care Consultants.*

That was the beginning of my efforts to make an impact on
the emerging field, but in order to truly understand my involvement, I must go back even further in my career to explain where
the seeds were originally sown.

From 1969 to 1973 I was an Educational Consultant for
Houghton Mifflin Company—a job which required considerable
travel. I married my first husband in 1972 and soon realized
that the excessive travel was no way to begin a new marriage.
Talk about work/life balance! And even though my territory was

changed to keep me at home more often in the New England area (my new home), I decided to change course. I left my consulting job at Houghton Mifflin, and I enrolled in a master's program at Lesley University in Cambridge, Massachusetts.

The cutting-edge master's degree program in Day Care Administration was designed and created by Belle Evans and her husband, George Saia, following the publication of Belle's groundbreaking book, *Infant Day Care*. Lesley University opened an on-campus center for infants through pre-school children, which became a lab school for the new program. Following my short-lived (four years) career teaching Junior High School English, I began to focus more on younger children in primary grades in my consulting work, and the day care program was a perfect fit for me and my future aspirations. With a master's degree in Day Care Administration, I was sure to be in on a rapidly growing emphasis on group care, particularly for infants and toddlers.

One of my first courses in the program was a child care licensing course taught by Gwen Morgan. This was the very first course ever taught in that discipline. I should emphasize once again that Boston was way ahead of the rest of the country when it came to providing child care services and regulations. I felt privileged to be in that program in the first place and very privileged, indeed, to become friendly with, and influenced by, the incomparable Gwen Morgan.

After finishing up that program and with my M.Ed. in hand, my first job was as the Director of the Child Study Center at Simmons College in Boston, Massachusetts. During my tenure in that position, I was responsible for transitioning the center from a half-day nursery school to a full day care program for pre-schoolers. It was a welcome change for the many professional mothers whose children were enrolled in the program, since they required additional hours of care for their children.

Soon after serving in that capacity, I became a mother myself, and began to understand first-hand the need for care, and the reality of the limited availability of comprehensive and quality care for young children. I used a variety of care solutions for my own children, including in-home care, day care home care, and other pre-school options that were accessible to me in my area. As my children grew and I remained a working mother, I continued to use extended day programs at their elementary school and other day care options.

I am a firm believer in the value of group care for the growth and development of young children. However, that care must be accessible, affordable, and above all, quality care, with trained caregivers. Study after study has attested to the gain children make especially regarding socialization, even for infants and toddlers.

During the years while my two children were very young, I worked part-time as an educational consultant, and taught Early Childhood Education courses at Bridgewater State College, Wheelock College, and Lesley College. My children were still in pre-school when I accepted the position as Assistant Professor of Early Childhood Education at Stonehill College. I served in that capacity for three years until deciding to start my consulting business. I remember very well those occasions when my own child care arrangements broke down and I needed to frantically leave Stonehill to drive back to Brookline (a forty-five-minute commute) to pick up my children from their pre-school, drive back to Stonehill, situate my children in the early childhood resource room that I had established for my students, and teach my next class!

Corporate Child Care Consultants

My personal journey on this winding road took many twists and turns under several different hats—from starting the journey as a self-employed professional and operating from a home office, to joining several partnerships, to being employed by giant corporations, until I ultimately decided to leave a growing organization headquartered in California. My decision to totally change direction was predicated on the assumption that the uphill battle was won to a certain extent, and the struggle might become even more difficult. Additionally, the economy began to change yet again as we approached the new millennium. My personal life changed, too, and I looked for a whole new challenge.

My First Consulting Contract—The Howard Johnson Company

In 1982 as interest grew in the development of employer-supported child care and the need for quality child care continued to grow, I found myself in the right place at the right time, so to speak.

After working with a graphic designer to create a logo and design business cards and brochures for my new business, I set up my home office on the third floor of our Brookline, Massachusetts, home, and began putting the word out that I was available. Elaine Dunn (my boss when I was at Simmons) and I had become close personal friends, and she was aware of my new venture. She put me in touch with Susan Good, who was an executive at *The Howard Johnson Company*, a company in the process of building new corporate headquarters in Quincy, Massachusetts.

G. Michael Hostage was named CEO of the company in 1981, after the London-based Imperial Group, Ltd. took ownership. He had been the former president of Marriott Corporation's restaurant operations. Mike was a forward-thinking kind of leader, who also happened to be the father of ten children. One of his daughters was a pre-school teacher and she pitched the idea to him to include a child care facility in the new building. The ingredients were there to convince Mike Hostage that an on-site child care facility was a good idea for the new location.

After an initial meeting with Susan and Mike, I was hired to conduct a needs assessment to determine if their workforce was interested in on-site child care, and if the parents would use it. I was off and running.

I created my first survey to assess the need for such a facility. It was rudimentary at best, but it got the job done. The purpose of a child care needs analysis is to survey the workforce and examine the current child care arrangements parents utilize, and to determine whether they would be inclined to use an on-site facility if one became available to them. The analysis of the survey also determined if there would be a cost/benefit for the company.

For that survey, the results were tabulated by hand!—a far cry from the more sophisticated needs analyses I conducted later on in my work/life career. Nevertheless, we got the data we needed and learned that the Howard Johnson parents often experienced break downs in their child care arrangements, or they managed on a regular basis with a band-aid type of arrangement that was haphazard at best. The data provided us with the desired results—the Howard Johnson employees were wholeheartedly in favor of an on-site child care facility—one that would include infants and toddlers and pre-school children.

I began working very closely with the Vice President of Human Resources and meeting with the architect of the new building. Under my guidance, ground floor space was allocated for the child care center, which consisted of the required thirty-five square feet of useable indoor space per child and seventy-five square feet of useable outdoor space per child, according to Massachusetts licensing regulations. We determined that the center would include an infant classroom, a toddler classroom, and a pre-school classroom for three- and four-year-olds. My responsibilities under the contract included the total design and development of the center (both indoor and outdoor); establishing a start-up and operating budget; hiring a center director and classroom teachers and assistants; purchasing all furniture, equipment, and toys; and creating a parent advisory board, which ultimately became the governing body for the center going forward.

It was a fabulous opportunity, and the center that we developed was first class. I was so proud. And it certainly got recognized. The media attention was notable. And Mike Hostage, the CEO, was proud of what we had accomplished. It was the best start I could ever have imagined for my little business.

The center opened in 1984. However, only a few years later, The Howard Johnson Company was sold again, and the company moved out of Quincy, Massachusetts. A group of parent volunteers took over the operation and management of the center and the center was re-named the Greater Quincy Child Care Center. GQCCC continues to operate today as a non-profit organization governed by a Board of Directors made up of parent volunteers and the center's Executive Director. The center has grown and thrived and is still run by the parent advisory board that we established in 1984.

Hill Holliday Connors Cosmopulos

My consulting business grew, and my reputation stretched beyond New England. I continued to communicate with both local child care experts, and with those advocating for employer-supported child care nationwide. Because I had opened The Howard Johnson Center and had successfully completed that contract, Hill Holliday Connors Cosmopulos, Boston's premier advertising agency, contacted me as they started thinking about a child care center—this time in downtown Boston. HHCC's offices were located in the John Hancock Tower, in the heart of downtown Boston. They knew that an on-site center was out of the question for them, so they began looking at nearby space to house their center.

Once again, I was hired to do a needs analysis, and design and develop the center after a location was selected, which was The First Baptist Church, two blocks away from the Hancock Tower. With my input, an architect was chosen to transform the ground floor space of the church hall into a child care facility. Andrea Leers of Leers Weinzapfel Associates became the architect on the project. I enjoyed my association with Andrea very much. She was innovative and creative in transforming a basic dull and raw space into an enchanting environment for toddlers and pre-school children. After a very successful grand opening of the center, Andrea presented me with a framed photo of the interior of the space—a cherished memento that I held onto for many years.

Throughout the contract I met regularly with Jack Connors, the CEO of HHCC. Through the years Jack became known as the most influential philanthropist in Boston, and also one of the most respected and prominent men in the area. He was proud that Hill Holliday opened the first corporate near-site child care center in downtown Boston. His wife, Eileen Connors, a member of my tennis team at the Mount Auburn Tennis Club, attended the grand opening of the center, along with Governor Mike Dukakis and other dignitaries. Media attention was tremendous once again, which, of course, added to its success.

Bronner Slosberg Humphrey

Because of my involvement with the Hill Holliday project, another major Boston advertising agency secured my services to investigate whether a work and family agenda could fit for them, too. That company was Bronner Slosberg Humphrey.

The advertising world creates an extremely high-pressured environment and an often overburdened workforce—one in which employees work very long hours. I conducted a needs analysis for them and several very in-depth focus groups in both their Boston and New York offices. Those focus groups were so revealing to me as their consultant, and equally revealing to the company higher-ups. We learned a great deal about how those young professionals coped with their stressful lives.

These focus groups, in particular, and the data collected from them, led to my becoming more educated in flexible work policies and other solutions to the work/life balance issues of employees, and what that meant for any workforce. We looked at job-sharing, work-at-home, sabbaticals, and lactation rooms for nursing mothers, as some examples. I worked very closely with Vice President Peggy Novello throughout the contract, with another good friendship resulting. I believe that Bronner Slosberg paved the way for high-paced work environments to pay more attention to providing resources and programs, which enabled key employees to stay on the job, instead of facing burnout and quitting.

ESCCN—Employer Supported Child Care Network

Many other businesses, organizations, and groups began forming across the nation and interest continued to rise in the provision of child care services or a work and family agenda. It became important to communicate with one another, share information, and help others to make the case to corporate CEOs and human resource managers. In New England many professionals saw the need for an organization to enable us to come together.

I joined with several others to start the *New England Employer-Supported Child Care Network*. My colleagues and I, who formed the original Board of Directors of the organization, were leaders within the community—all doing our part to advance the cause. The board included: Martha Izzi, Regional Director of the Women's Bureau of the U. S. Department of Labor; Sue Halloran, Director of the Government Center Child Development Center; Martha Poehler, Researcher at the U.S. Department of Transportation; Stanley Kuziel, Executive Director of The Prospect Hill Child Care Center in Waltham, Massachusetts; and me, President of Corporate Child Care Consultants. Roger Brown, Founder and President of Bright Horizons, joined our board after a while. And Joan Heminway, attorney at Skadden

Arps in Boston became a legal consultant, assisting us in structuring the organization and developing by-laws.

Although not a member of our board, Patricia Cronin, played a huge role in the activities of the ESCCN, too. Pat served as assistant to Evelyn Murphy, who was Massachusetts Secretary of Economic Affairs from 1983–1986. When Evelyn was elected Massachusetts Lieutenant Governor under Mike Dukakis in 1987, Joe Alviani was named Secretary of Economic Affairs, and our connection with that office continued. Pat Cronin played an integral part in helping the ESCCN link with governmental departments and we valued her friendship and input. Sadly, however, Pat Cronin, has passed away.

We held monthly meetings with speakers from various entities. Our membership grew each year. The members who attended those monthly meetings came from all over New England to share experiences and information. ESCCN emerged as a critical resource for those who required more support, as the development of employer-supported child care services grew in the region.

The board met each month at a Boston hotel for a breakfast meeting to plan the agenda for the next meeting. We did treat ourselves well! We alternated between The Ritz Carlton and The Boston Harbor Hotel for those breakfast meetings. I clearly remember one such breakfast at The Ritz when I looked across the room and there was Uncle Ted (my husband's uncle, Theodore Anzalone), City Assessor, having breakfast with then Mayor of Boston Kevin White. When Uncle Ted noticed me, he came over to our table, and with a wry smile asked, "What are you doing here?!" Those breakfasts linger as fond memories—as our friendships grew, and we realized that we were providing a much-needed resource within the region.

Fortunately for us, The ESCCN group caught the attention of *The Boston Globe* columnist Juliet Brudney, who wrote a weekly column called "Living with Work." Juliet Brudney became a good friend of the Network. She often attended our meetings and she interviewed and quoted me many times in her column. Juliet was also a fellow Vineyarder, and I recalled many times when we would meet on the ferry from Woods Hole to Martha's Vineyard. She was helpful in moving the dial forward in New England. Juliet is another who has departed this earth.

ESCCN became the first regional organization with its sole purpose being the expansion, support, and foundation of child care services in the corporate arena. My fellow board members and I each had a personal stake in moving the agenda forward and we did good work together. We also became fast friends and were instrumental in one another's success, and we have remained friends and are in contact with one another to this day.

National Conferences

As the field began to grow and new organizations popped up to provide services, we depended on those resources coming together at national conferences to learn and to be recognized.

In 1985 *Working Mother Magazine* began compiling a list of the 100 Best Companies for Working Mothers, and they held an annual conference to announce the winners. That conference and the award winners became an important resource for all of us. The conference always drew major speakers who were influential in 'talking the talk', and 'walking the walk.'

At one of those conferences the keynote speaker was none other than Bill Clinton, who was Governor of Arkansas at the time. It was well before he made a run for the presidency, and he was looked upon as a forward-thinking politician who cared about children. I clearly remember, however, and we all agreed . . . his speech was very long and very boring!

Drexel University

Drexel University in Philadelphia, Pennsylvania, convened a conference in the mid-80s that concentrated on the work/family agenda, which helped to move attention into a more national realm. Many of the aforementioned players were either attendees or speakers at that conference. Drexel sponsored a second conference on the same topics a few years later.

NAEYC—National Association for the Education of Young Children

NAEYC continued to offer a work/family track at their national conference for many years. As a lifetime member of the organization, I presented many workshops that highlighted my involvement in the field, and it was at those conferences each year that I reaffirmed my association and friendship with many colleagues from around the country. It became such an important vehicle to promote the cause and for us to get together.

Northeastern University National Conference on Work/Life

In 1993 I was fortunate to be in a position to become associated with the Human Resource Office at Northeastern University in Boston, Massachusetts. Jane Scarborough and I met many times until I ultimately convinced her to secure the required funding to sponsor a major national conference that would highlight all of the work/life programs that were continuing to be developed throughout the country. In fact, it was the very first time that the term "Work/Life" was used in the title of a national conference, rather than "Work/Family." And I modestly consider that as one of my personal achievements, for, from then on, the term "Work/Life" became the norm.

I was Chair of the conference, and I was responsible for securing all the speakers, outlining the agenda and workshops, and handling all logistics. The conference was held at Northeastern, was widely attended, and helped us achieve another milestone.

AWLP Conferences

The Alliance of Work/Life Professionals (detailed more fully in a following section), convened a national conference for over ten years. As I stated in the Acknowledgments, my involvement in the creation of the AWLP is one of my major accomplishments within the field. I loved every minute working with my friends and colleagues on this organization, particularly partaking in the design of its annual conference. I was fortunate enough to be named Chair of the conference in both 1997 and 1998, when the conference was held at the Hotel Del Coronado in San Diego, California, and the Intercontinental Hotel in Miami, Florida, respectively. These conferences grew in attendance as each year progressed and we enjoyed an increasing membership year after year. We also secured many first-rate keynote speakers. More on that later.

Al Gore's Work/Family Conference in Nashville, Tennessee

During the first Clinton administration, Vice President Al Gore became a staunch proponent of work/family initiatives, so much so that he convened a major conference in his home state of Tennessee. A contingent group from our AWLP Board of Directors was invited to attend the conference. We were very surprised and delighted to be in attendance when President Bill Clinton and First Lady Hillary Rodham Clinton, along with Vice President Al Gore and his wife Tipper Gore, appeared on stage together. It was a mesmerizing vision to see both couples up there espousing the very topics we were so passionate about. We were even invited to a barbecue at Al Gore's ranch. Wow, were we in at that point! Al Gore posed for a photo with a few of my colleagues and me.

Picnic following Family Conference in Nashville, Tennessee, 1995.
Ann Vincola, MaryEllen Gornick, Barbara Adolf, Vice President
Al Gore, Madeline Fried, Roger Neugebauer.

4

My Partners and Clients

A fter successfully completing the contracts with my first few clients, I continued to learn and expand my knowledge and reputation—as the field began to do the same. I was very fortunate to be able to attend conferences, travel extensively, and meet with others across the country. Soon I became a recognized expert within the burgeoning field, and I was asked to speak and participate in conferences and workshops both nationally and regionally. I was contacted by the media regularly and was often quoted in *The Wall Street Journal* or *The New York Times* or *The Boston Globe*.

As mentioned earlier, I operated under several different corporate names, and with some of my colleagues, at critical times during my career as a work/life consultant. Because of the changing nature of the field, and the growth of service providers, it was clear that one needed bench strength in order to compete, and I sought partnerships which could provide me with additional resources. So, from a one-woman operation to joining forces with other like-minded individuals or organizations, I felt I could be more effective with partners by my side.

My little office on the third floor of my home in Brookline, Massachusetts, started closing in on me. I operated from there for about three years until my husband offered me the use of space that he had purchased in a renovated warehouse on Congress Street on the waterfront in Boston. The space sat unused, and it became the perfect location for me from which to work. Prior to the move, my home office had been adequate, but by then I needed to hire an assistant, and I required a more appropriate space to receive clients, colleagues, or the media, as my client list continued to expand.

Summa Associates

The first group I joined was called Summa Associates. The seed for the creation of this company was sown when I met with Sandy Burud, Stephanie Fanjul, Karen Woodford, and Nadine Mathis at Nadine's vacation home in Sedona, Arizona. We had so much fun thinking about what an alliance could mean to our respective businesses—so much so that we got a little giddy thinking of the possibilities. One cute little story developed when we discovered that both Stephanie and I had purchased the exact same dress at our respective local Marshall's store, and we had brought the dress with us. We even talked about purchasing the same dress for Sandy, Nadine, and Karen, and we planned on wearing them to the next event we all attended together. How silly. But it seemed like a good idea at the time!

We continued to brainstorm on what our new alliance could provide by having a west coast and east coast presence and bringing together some of the leaders in the new field. Barbara Adolf and Karol Rose of Adolf and Rose in New York City were

Business merger discussion, Sedona, Arizona, 1985.
Stephanie Fanjul, Nadine Mathis, Karen Woodford,
Sandy Burud, Ann Vincola.

approached to join us as well, but they ultimately declined. And Stephanie determined that it was not the right time for her. So, the initial new partnership began with Sandy and her partner, Cindy Ransom, in Pasadena, California; Karen and Nadine in Tempe, Arizona; and me in Boston, Massachusetts.

We researched our name and settled on Summa Associates— *summa* meaning the highest, the best, the greatest, as in *summa cum laude*. After all, we did consider ourselves the very top in the field. And so, it began. I don't think we ever completed a contract together, or if we did, I don't remember it. What I do remember, however, is that we spent an inordinate amount of time planning—printing brochures, discussing our rollout, agreeing on services provided, etc. I really don't think we had gotten any further than that.

I had developed a connection and relationship with a consultant at KPMG Peat Marwick in Boston, one of the Big Six Accounting firms, as we began putting our new company together. Following several meetings that I had with one of the

Partners at Peat Marwick, my relationship with the firm continued to grow, and the Boston office became interested in our group. It was decided that it might be worth our while for all the principals to come to Boston to see whether there was a fit and where that might lead.

Sandy, Cindy, Karen, and Nadine came to Boston and stayed at my house to attend a meeting at Peat Marwick to discuss future possible alliances. I was thrilled to host my new partners in my Brookline home; however, I was a little nervous as to how my husband would react to having my colleagues stay with us. Although he seemed to be supportive of my professional efforts, he often acted in a way that somewhat thwarted those efforts. I often wonder whether if I had more support at home in terms of my professional life, perhaps I would have achieved an even higher degree of success.

I was generally not happy with the entire visit because a few situations occurred that were uncomfortable for me and for the others as well. Perhaps it was a foreboding of an unsuccessful alliance.

After the meeting at Peat Marwick, I remember Sandy being very excited. As we left the office, and discussed the meeting in the elevator, Sandy declared, "I think they are going to make us all Partners!" Boy, was she off the mark. Following my efforts to develop the initial relationship in Boston, negotiations between our group and KPMG moved to California, and Sandy and Cindy were charged with taking over from there to communicate with a California Peat Marwick Partner. That partner was not convinced that an alliance with us was the best thing for Peat Marwick, and any potential deal fell through.

The demise of that potential liaison led to disagreements and inner struggles within our partnership, particularly as to who should assume the leadership role. Sandy invariably thought it should be her since she had the greatest national recognition at the time. But I had my doubts about that because I felt leadership within a group was not part of her skill set. And I became even more doubtful about her steering the ship, after I saw how the California contingent bungled any potential deal with Peat Marwick.

Conference call after conference call followed with difficult conversations and many tears. As the scenario became unbearable for me, I withdrew from the group. I was not interested in wasting time listening to Sandy cry on the phone each time we talked. I do believe that it was a question of five female egos vying for the top dog position, which never could work. It was a period of time when women were just beginning to learn how to work together and support one another for the greater good. Our little group was just not there yet.

Sandy eventually decided to withdraw from Summa Associates, too. Karen and Nadine held on to the name and continued to operate under that heading. Karen Woodford is President of Summa Associates today.

It was not a good break-up. And, honestly, our relationship was never the same again. What started out with huge hopes of great achievement and a giddy high, ended up with hurt feelings and bad vibes. My relationship with Sandy never really healed. The whole episode was a huge disappointment for me—an alliance which could have had such great potential and influence on the entire field, but couldn't get off the ground.

The Benefits Resource Group

The economy was good from 1983 to 1990—the initial growth years of our movement, but then the nation experienced another recession. The 1990 to 1991 downturn was exacerbated by several external factors such as the Persian Gulf crises, the savings-and-loan collapse, and continued job cutbacks. This recession lasted from July 1990 to March 1991, and it had a distinct impact on what was happening in corporate America. The recession also coincided with a slowing down for my business, too, and I began looking for other ways to compete within the marketplace.

Enter a very decent human being to the rescue, for a group of us looking for direction—Woolsey S. Conover. Woolsey was the recently retired Founder and Principal of Consolidated Group Trust headquartered in Framingham, Massachusetts, an employee benefits administration company with over 800 employees. After retiring, and before he became a board member and trustee of several prestigious organizations, Woolsey looked for a purpose, and he wound up helping a group of entrepreneurs form a consortium. I became a member of that consortium, which we named *The Benefits Resource Group.*

The other members of the group were Rick Beineke, a health benefits professional; Gretchen Von Merring, a wellness activist; and Manny Chrobak, an employee benefits expert and a former employee at Woolsey's company, Consolidated Group. With me focusing on the work/life and dependent care aspect of a full employee benefits package, we marketed our consortium as a service for human resource executives to blend employee benefits into a cohesive package.

We operated as independent contractors within the consortium, but we coordinated our efforts with the others to promote and integrate the concept of combining benefits. And Woolsey paid the bills! We took office space in Natick, Massachusetts, at first, and then moved into a larger building in Framingham, Massachusetts. Woolsey served as the glue to keep us together and provided us guidance as well as financial stability.

We enjoyed moderate success considering the state of the economy at the time and were recognized regionally, particularly within *NEHRA, the Northeast Human Resource Association.* I served on several committees for the organization, particularly its annual conference committee, and I presented at that conference, too.

I completed contracts with several regional clients with The Benefits Resource Group, but it was a time of essentially treading water rather than moving forward. I will be eternally grateful to Woolsey, however, for keeping us all afloat during a difficult period. He even paid each of us a Christmas bonus each year out of the goodness of his heart—and deep pockets!

In my research for this book and checking back on some of the people I worked with, I learned that Rick Beineke passed away in 2017.

Coopers & Lybrand

By 1993, after spending over ten years as a consultant in the work/family-work/life arena, I had made a name for myself, and my expertise was recognized and sought. I also continued to work closely with my colleagues on the national level to promote our agenda. Both The Alliance and the AWLP were in its infancy by that time, and my attention was focused on the development and growth of those organizations as well as on my own business.

About that time, I somehow appeared on the radar screen of Larry Schumer, the Managing Partner at *Coopers & Lybrand's Human Resource Advisory Group*, after meeting one another at a NEHRA conference. Larry was the youngest person ever to be named managing partner of HRA at Coopers. Larry invited me to breakfast on a few occasions and we discussed our respective roles, while at the same time he tried to convince me to join his organization. It took a lot of thinking and soul searching on my part, plus several months, before I said yes.

By 1994 I was named *National Director of Work/Life Consulting* for Coopers & Lybrand's Human Resource Advisory Group. I couldn't be happier about the rollout and announcement of my new position. My office was at International Place in Boston, and I was riding high as I entered my office each day on the tenth floor of that beautiful and imposing building. It was a period in my career whereby I was surrounded by brilliant colleagues, extraordinary resources, incredible opportunities, and . . . I was paid a very nice salary . . . and bonus!

Being named National Director of Work/Life Consulting for Coopers & Lybrand was groundbreaking at that time. I was the first work/life consultant hired by a Big Six accounting firm to provide assistance in the development of work/life programs for their clients. It was a big deal for me and for them. The Big Six then consisted of Deloitte & Touche, KPMG Peat Marwick, Ernst & Young, Price Waterhouse, Arthur Anderson, and Coopers & Lybrand. Through mergers and acquisitions the landscape has changed significantly, and the accounting firms later assumed an identity within the work/life arena, particularly Deloitte & Touche.

I distinctly recall overhearing Dana Friedman telling another colleague at one of the Drexel University conferences: "Did you hear—Ann Vincola has been hired by Coopers!" It was big news—and I was thrilled and pretty excited about my new role. Larry Schumer provided me with the internal support necessary to propel me into this new stratosphere. It was another world entirely for me and I loved being part of it.

I completed several contracts with major clients during my tenure at C&L, including a very comprehensive needs analysis for Burger King Corporation. I made the trip to their headquarters in Miami, Florida, and submitted our proposal. Larry joined me by flying down and back (a three-hour flight each way from Boston) in one day to convince their CEO and VP of HR that we were the right choice for them. I enjoyed working with their team and we achieved a successful outcome. It was one of my favorite all-time contracts, and I became very fond of the people at Burger King with whom I worked.

My biggest success while at C&L, however, was conducting a performance audit for the Smart Start Program (early childhood centers) for the State of North Carolina. My good friend, Stephanie Fanjul, at the time serving as Director of the state-run Head Start Program called Smart Start, had the inside track and knowledge beforehand that an RFP (Request for Proposal) would be coming, and she gave a few of us a heads-up. The contract was to conduct a "performance audit" of the entire program to determine how each county in North Carolina spent the money they were allotted. Because it was a state mandated and controlled program, there was a certain political focus to it, which became apparent. Since the state was spending a total of $30 million on it annually, the legislature wanted to know how their money was being spent and whether it was worth it!

I knew instantly that this contract could be a perfect way to coordinate my position within the field with the resources and strength of C&L, and I could write a winning proposal—a particular strength of mine. It was a half-a-million-dollar contract—unheard of in the work/life arena thus far. I wrote the proposal and submitted and presented it along with a C&L Partner from our Raleigh office. Of course, none of us really knew what a "performance audit" should consist of, but somehow, we got the point across that we were the right firm to conduct the evaluation.

Since the project consisted of evaluating all of the Smart Start early childhood centers throughout the state, I decided to enlist the aid of several of my friends and colleagues, all of whom were child care experts, who could easily conduct the necessary evaluations. I shared the contract with Karen Woodford and Nadine Mathis of Summa Associates, Mary Ellen Gornick of The CPA Group, and Madeline Fried of Fried and Sher. The fact that I could bring in all of those experts won us the contract. I remember calling Larry as I was on my way to the airport to fly back to Boston after our presentation to tell him: "We did it! We got the contract!!!"

I served as project manager for the audit, by developing an overall strategic plan, organizing, and overseeing the evaluations, and writing a cohesive final report. I had three young consultants at C&L work with me on the contract. To this day, it was the very best experience I've ever had and the best example of a smooth and effective display of cooperation and hard work. Paul

Neveu, Eileen Schneider, and Sarah Callabria were the best of the best. They crisscrossed the state of North Carolina and as novices in the field, they learned a hell of a lot about child care. All three have gone on to have exemplary careers in the human resource arena, and Paul is now CEO of BPAS, a retirement and employee benefits firm, and I have been delighted to reconnect with him. Almost thirty years after working with him as a young consultant, I can honestly say that he is the embodiment of what a good CEO should be.

All went extremely well as we conducted the audit until I was dumbstruck by being sabotaged by one of my so-called friends—whom I had generously brought into the contract, by the way! Nadine Mathis Basha called the new managing partner at C&L's Boston HRA division, Ernie Glickman, and complained about my supervision of the contract. It was utter nonsense because we did an excellent job, and I clearly handled it all very well. I can only assume that Nadine was jealous that I got the contract in the first place, and she couldn't understand why they didn't! Talk about backstabbing.

I had to do some gentle maneuvering and enlisted the help of my other colleagues on the project to quell the damage. We presented the final report to the North Carolina legislature, and we were secure in a job well done. My bonus that year was a hefty one!

The internal support that I clearly needed with Larry Schumer as Managing Partner of HRA didn't last very long. For unknown reasons, Larry was relocated to the C&L London office and a new managing partner took over. Coopers & Lybrand had recently acquired a consulting organization—Harbridge House, and Ernie Glickman was named the new HRA Managing Partner.

On the one hand, it was good for me because Harbridge House added a diversity consulting arm to our HRA group, which fit naturally with my work/life agenda, but Ernie was a very different kind of leader than Larry had been. And Larry was the guy who brought me into the fold, and I missed his support. Larry was one leader I knew would 'always have my back.' The change presented new challenges for me; however, I must admit that Ernie did stick up for me during the Smart Start debacle, when he was contacted by one of my 'friends.'

And Ernie also supported me when there was a decision to be made as to whether the diversity and work/life consulting practices should be joined into one practice. Prior to that I had been introduced to the Harbridge House diversity team—two women who had a great deal of experience in the field. We began working together and I was very pleased to be included in many client diversity training and sexual harassment workshops. It seemed like a natural fit. But, once again, here we were with three women vying for the top spot—never a comfortable situation. In my experience, professional women of my generation did not do well when competing with one another. Observing my daughter in her work situations, I think it is different today. I believe that women have learned to work better together and support one another in a once male-dominated world.

Ernie secretly shared with me that he was supporting me to be practice leader. That did not sit well with the others, and when they found out, chaos followed, with a lot of behind-the-scenes manipulation going on. Ultimately the practices did not merge, because there was more happening within the HRA Group at the time that was far more important and challenging than our struggles to become practice leader.

In 1996 big changes were occurring in the world of the Big Six Accounting firms. Mergers and acquisitions were happening regularly. Coopers & Lybrand acquired Kwasha Lipton, a small employee benefits consulting firm located just across the George Washington bridge in Fort Lee, New Jersey, and that had big implications for me. Why?

Well, because one of my fellow work/life consultants had been brought into Kwasha Lipton as a partner a few years prior to the merger, and she and I were not always 'on the same page,' let's say. Karol Rose and I pretended to like one another and be friends, but in my circle, she was called the *Barracuda*. The merger set up an interesting dynamic and dilemma for me. I was operating as the National Director of Work/Life Consulting for C&L, but I was not a partner. In the accounting world, the hierarchy did not include the level of Director—that was just a title. I did not have partner status; however, I enjoyed many other partner benefits, like a bigger office, staff, and salary. But Karol would have seniority over me once the merger was completed because of her partner status.

We played at making it work for a short period of time, but it was uncomfortable to say the least. So much so, that when I was approached by Work/Life Benefits, a vendor company, I jumped ship. I accepted the offer "I couldn't refuse," but I didn't tell anyone until I gave my two weeks' notice to Ernie, shocking Karol, and everyone else at C&L.

Not very long after that (1998), after I had departed the firm, another big change occurred—the merger of Coopers & Lybrand and Price Waterhouse. I didn't pay too much attention to that since I was doing quite well at my new company, but I did learn that Karol did not remain at Price Waterhouse Coopers for very long after the merger took place.

Before I tell you about my time at Work/Life Benefits, there is another interesting, and to me, rather amusing story that occurred during my last few months at C&L. The new practice leaders were running a different type of organization—or so it seemed to me. Ernie and his fellow partners (all men by the way) were faced with a unique dilemma. It seemed that a partner in Connecticut had contacted our office because Ted Kennedy Jr. was interested in working at Coopers & Lybrand, and he needed to be interviewed. The Connecticut office pushed it on to the Boston office. All of this was rather secretive because any apparent preferential treatment was a no-no.

None of the partners in our Boston office were interested in being the interviewer. So, they came to me. Would I do them the favor of meeting with Ted Kennedy Jr. and interview him for a position in the Human Resource Advisory Group of Coopers & Lybrand? What? Me? I couldn't believe they were asking me to do this. Me . . . not being a partner, of course! I guess it had to do with politics, and these men decided that I would be a better fit to meet with the young Kennedy, rather than any of them taking on the task.

And it all had to be approached in a rather undercover manner. When young Ted came to the office, I met him downstairs in the lobby of the building and escorted him up to the ninth floor conference room where the interview took place. Our office was on the tenth floor, but he was not to be seen there.

We spent a delightful hour and a half talking to one another. He was charming. He asked good questions, and I was able to give him proper insight as to what life was like at C&L. He was very genuine. He talked about his family and why he wanted a change and why working at C&L might fit for him. He never joined the firm. I'm not sure what direction he followed, but I felt privileged to have spent time with him. And that is my little story about how I interviewed Ted Kennedy Jr.

Work/Life Benefits

As my days at C&L were coming to end, I knew exactly what I was going to do, because I was presented with a very agreeable offer from Nigel Ayers, the CEO of Work/Life Benefits, a dependent care vendor company. Originally called *The Voucher Corporation*, providing dependent care subsidies for corporate clients, and owned by French company ACCOR, INTERNATIONAL, the company had morphed into Work/Life Benefits, and Nigel, a Brit, was hired as CEO. They were, however, lacking a consulting division, and Nigel was foresighted enough to realize that consulting contracts could provide another revenue stream, which would make them more competitive in the marketplace.

Earlier that year my good friend, Carey Fleming, a longtime employee at The Voucher Corporation and fellow AWLP Board member, suggested that we have dinner together when Nigel was in Boston. It was a very positive encounter and delightful meeting, and I wished Nigel well as he began his new role and job in Orange County, California. I could never have predicted then that I would soon be working with them.

In February of the following year, I was serving as Chair of the AWLP Conference, at the Hotel Del Coronado in San Diego, California. I was favorably positioned at that conference in my role as Conference Chair, to be very noticeable and constantly visible at a very prestigious event. So much so, that Nigel was duly impressed, and he vowed then and there that I would soon become part of their team! I was invited to breakfast with Nigel and his Senior Vice President, Reggie Gitlin, the day the conference ended. Meeting with them needed to be kind of a secret arrangement, so as not to alert the work/life community that an interesting connection might covertly be in the works. I remember that we sort of sneaked around and didn't want anyone to know that we were talking about me joining them.

The result of that breakfast meeting was "the offer I couldn't refuse!" The deal included an excellent salary, a more substantial annual bonus, and the establishment of a Boston office and staff for me. They also encouraged my continued involvement on the national scene with AWLP and The Alliance. I accepted the offer then and there and I told them that it would take me only two weeks to give my notice at Coopers & Lybrand and be ready to start with them. Smiles, handshakes, and hugs followed as we noticed Ed Houghton of Pitney Bowes Corporation, who was soon to become a member of the AWLP Board, sitting at another table in the corner of the restaurant, looking on quizzically wondering if he had just witnessed something major happening!

The tension and the pain in my lower back that had begun as the conference was ending, because of the heavy load I was carrying, miraculously disappeared right there at that breakfast. I had my way out of my dilemma at C&L and it was time to move on. Later that afternoon as all the conference participants were preparing to leave the Hotel Del and fly back home, I met Reggie at an agreed-upon location (a bank of wall phones) where she surreptitiously slipped a plane ticket into my hand. The ticket was for my return trip to California—exactly two weeks from that day, when I would officially become Senior Vice President of Work/Life Benefits, and the big announcement would be made.

Once I wrapped things up at C&L, I was eager to begin my new role as part of senior management at Work/Life Benefits, along with Nigel and Reggie, and then get started opening our Boston office. We rented space in the Prudential Tower, which was in walking distance of my home in the South End of Boston. We had enough space for my executive office, two other smaller offices, and a large area that served as a conference room and a wall of file cabinets to house my ever-increasing resources and project files. We rented furniture and computers, telephone system, and copy machine, and I hired staff. We were off to an excellent start. The media rollout for my new position was aggressive and bold. The work/life field was enthusiastic. It was big news in the work/life world.

I knew what lay ahead for me, but I also knew that it wasn't going to be easy. Once again, I lacked the bench strength to undertake complicated consulting contracts, once awarded one, although the corporate and sales staff provided some support. At the corporate level we hired my good friend Pam Kerns, who had considerable experience working in HR at Duke Power and then at The Partnership Group. It was a period of time that I was so pleased to be working with friends like Pam and Carey Fleming, plus a great team of sales people who were still operating on the subsidy side of the company, like Donna Martino and Rob Cinco. It was fun. Pam Kerns joined me from time to time at proposal meetings to help make the pitch, as consulting opportunities arose.

We were clicking along, and we were successful at securing several new consulting clients. My Boston crew did quite well, too, and we grew. The climate seemed to be changing, however. There was more talk about 'return on investment (ROI)' and culture change within organizations, and, to me, a shift was beginning—a shift in the perception of the value of work/life programs within an employee benefits package. Throughout the 90s the U.S. experienced an economic boom, but as the millennium approached, there was a decided slowing down in the job market prior to 2000 as well as a decline in the economy until The Great Recession of 2008.

I enjoyed three years as Senior Vice President at Work/Life Benefits, and I spent my time traveling to clients and to our corporate headquarters in Orange County, California. Nigel was an inspirational leader and the potential for growth and expansion of the company was clearly evident.

At the end of my first year with the company, I was asked to plan a two-day mini conference in Boston for the higher-ups from ACCOR who wanted to visit their U.S. subsidiary. I so enjoyed that assignment preparing for the meeting, which was held at the Boston Harbor Hotel. We presented a formal outline of our goals, services, programs, staff, and financial outlook to the powers-that-be at ACCOR. We were proud of where we stood then, and the anticipation of the future that lay ahead for us as an organization. And I was proud of how I organized the entire visit—including dinner at the finest French restaurant in Boston! We believed that we presented an exceptional outlook for future success.

We continued to achieve our goals until ACCOR began changing direction, and suddenly became exceedingly punitive with its little American subsidiary. That is why we were shocked beyond belief when ACCOR pulled the plug!

A consultant was hired in California to oversee the company's financials, and Nigel began to see the handwriting on the wall until he knew that his job was in jeopardy. I will never forget his phone call to me—"I've been sacked!" It was shocking—earth-shattering to all of us, especially to me, after such fanfare when I was brought onboard. And it was quick and vicious. I was told to beware of what would follow. The consultant, Chris Newton, was on his way to Boston to close down our office. Pam Kerns and Carey Fleming were told to come to the Boston office, and as we all sat in my conference room, we were told that we were all FIRED! Pam recalled that she and Carey went immediately to a bar in Boston to moan and commiserate, and as she relayed to me: "Three martinis later . . . Carey's parents needed to come and pick us up because we'd had so much to drink, we knew we couldn't drive home. It was horrible."

Chris Newton met with me personally and informed me that he was hired "to stop the bleeding!" I was given two weeks' severance and no bonus or anything else. I was not allowed to break down the office myself, nor could I speak with my staff. It was cruel and unusual behavior, which none of us deserved. I only wish that I had hired an employment lawyer to examine my rights at the time and to represent my interests, rather than rely on my attorney husband, who had no experience with employment law. And I felt horrible for my staff, all of whom I had carefully selected. They were left totally out in the cold. The last person I hired was directed by Chris to close down the office. It was awful. And everyone was miserable at how we were being treated with no forewarning.

Nigel was on his way back to the U.K. and Chris Newton became the CEO at the California office. Work/Life Benefits returned to providing dependent care vouchers for corporate clients as its only service, and I was out of a job. Would I go back to being a sole proprietor?

A very sad outcome to the entire Work/Life Benefits debacle was that later that year, Chris Newton was on his way to Boston in preparation of moving his family east to establish residency in Boston and open a new ACCOR office . . . on September 11, 2001. Chris was on the plane that hit the Pentagon on that fateful day.

Knowledge Beginnings

Prior to the miserable scenario at Work/Life Benefits playing itself out, both Pam Kerns and Carey Fleming had begun to develop a relationship with Elanna Yallow, President and CEO of Children's Discovery Centers, a for-profit chain of child care facilities based in California. Elanna was beginning an association with the newly formed company, Knowledge Beginnings, a subsidiary of Knowledge Universe, and CDC was subsequently acquired by Knowledge Universe.

Pam, Carey, and I all remember being so miserable during the last few months at WLB. Pam remembers that Reggie kept trying to contact them on their cell phones, but she couldn't find them. It was a confusing time, and we were not certain as to what to do. Somehow, we knew the ax was about to fall. So, it was a welcome idea when we learned that Carey had devised 'a plan.'

Carey Fleming secured a meeting for me, Pam Kerns, and Carey, with Elanna Yallow at her office in San Rafael, California. At that meeting we discussed a deal to bring the three of us into the Knowledge Beginnings family, and for me to create and head their new Work/Life Consulting Division. We still had not been 'let go' at Work/Life Benefits, but the foreboding signs were evident.

I was between a rock and a hard place—expecting that I might be in need of a job soon. However, joining forces with a company whose for-profit child care philosophy that did not quite jibe with my perception of quality child care, was another thing altogether. Ultimately, I was offered a new job and a new opportunity to make a difference, and as it turned out, I was not in a position to refuse, after what transpired at Work/Life Benefits. Knowledge Beginnings pursued me aggressively. Pam was also offered a position, but Carey decided to move on in another direction.

In 1997 Larry Ellison of Oracle Corporation, and Michael and Lowell Milken of The Milken Family Foundation founded Knowledge Universe with $500 million, for the purpose of creating a corporation based on education—from cradle to grave—as it turned out. The company initially purchased Leap Frog, a toy manufacturer, and Nobel Education. Then in 1998 the company bought a chain of for-profit child care centers including Children's Discovery Centers and KinderCare Learning Centers. Three of the richest men in the universe entered the field of education as a for-profit enterprise, and I was offered an opportunity to join them! And as I mentioned earlier, they aggressively pursued me. In fact, I was shocked when I was met on the plane while traveling back to Boston by Elanna Yallow, who miraculously appeared in the first-class seat next to me. How did she manage that!? More pressure!

I honestly can't remember many details of the negotiations or how the deal was packaged, because I was still confused and hurt over the uncomfortable manner in which my time at Work/

Life Benefits ended. I was still reeling over that, and anything else seemed very enticing. And I was being wined and dined by the powers-that-be at Knowledge Universe.

Let's back up a bit. Michael Milken began his career in the 70s at Drexel Burnham Lambert and is known for his role in the development of the market for high-yield bonds (junk bonds), and for his conviction and sentence following a guilty plea on felony charges for violating U.S. securities law. He spent twenty-two months in jail and was fined $200 million.

He was unfortunately diagnosed with prostate cancer immediately upon his release from prison. It was then that Michael and his brother Lowell founded Knowledge Universe along with their friend Larry Ellison, co-founder and Executive Chairman of Oracle Corporation, the American computer technology company. Michael became obsessed with his health and well-being and even wrote a cookbook about healthy eating. He beat the cancer and Knowledge Universe continued to buy up education companies.

While being pursued by Knowledge Universe as they created Knowledge Beginnings, I never got to meet Michael or Larry, but I did meet Lowell. This was a corporate environment that I was not used to—to say the least. I have met with many CEOs of companies, both large and small, but this was different. It reeked money! I can still see the most perfect bowl of fresh fruit sitting on the small conference table in Lowell Milken's office. It was just he and I at that meeting, as we discussed the direction Knowledge Beginnings would be taking, and he encouraged me to join them.

I was also invited to dinner at Spago, Wolfgang Puck's famous restaurant in Malibu, California, by Ron Packard, who ultimately was named CEO of Knowledge Beginnings. Ron's goal at that dinner was to convince me to come on board, which would "make him very happy!" And on another occasion Pam and I were asked to attend a luncheon at the Milken Family Foundation headquarters. We dined on Michael Milken's healthy array of fresh foods as we discussed the future, and how Knowledge Beginnings would grow to become a major player in the work/life and child care arena.

I was to be their *Rainmaker*, charged to bring in corporate clients for big bucks contracts. Hmmm—that was going to be a hard order to fill, especially since work/life was not necessarily a money-making proposition in the first place. It was not a perfect fit, by any means, and I was skeptical, because Knowledge Beginnings' overall philosophy was not necessarily in sync with my general child care fundamentals. But I bit the bullet and took a chance and said yes!

I set up my home office once again, but this time I was given a generous budget to purchase new furniture and redesign and redecorate a room in our Boston South End five-story townhouse. It was a quick transition from the Work/Life Benefits office space at the Prudential Tower, and all my files were successfully moved over. Two new phone lines were installed as well. I have to say that the transition went as smoothly as possible, and I was pleased with my set up for the time being. I was still doing considerable travel, and by that time I had accumulated so many frequent flyer miles that I always traveled first class. And, oh yes, I had a car service to transport me from my home to the airport and pick me up wherever I landed. I was traveling back and forth from Detroit and New York a lot during that time frame to see clients. I couldn't complain about the company perks!

I continued servicing the few clients with whom I was still under contract, and we were in the running for several new projects for which we submitted proposals. But it was soon evident to me that I couldn't do it all by myself. I didn't have any assistance within the organization to provide a sense of strength to accomplish the many tasks that the new projects required, and we lost several opportunities. I soon became very frustrated, and I felt that we were not heading in a positive direction.

At the same time, my national reputation had grown to such an extent, as I continued to publish many articles in HR journals and other media, that I was approached by start-up companies, with deep pockets and high aspirations, to become a board member of several new organizations. In fact, announcements were made in the press, but, frankly, I can't even remember the names of these new companies. I do remember, however, being aggressively courted by these start-ups. One group invited me to a gala event on the floor of the stock exchange in New York City, while hosting me at The Waldorf Astoria Hotel, and another company visited with me at my apartment in Boston several times hoping to get me to accept their invitation to join their new board. Apparently, I was a good catch then! It seemed that everyone wanted to be in on the action. Work/Life was the place to be! That added to my frustration, too.

This was also the time of the Dot-Com Bubble which lasted from 1995 to 2000. The Dot-Com Bubble was a period during which rampant speculation and bullish investment led to the overvaluation (and subsequent crash) of the young internet technology industry on Wall Street. Many internet related start-up companies appeared on the scene, including many work/life companies. Investors pumped money into these internet start-ups in hopes that the fledgling companies would soon turn a profit. But instead, the bubble burst. And that was another foreboding to me that it was time to get out.

In the meantime, Knowledge Universe/Knowledge Beginnings continued to acquire companies and grow exponentially, albeit with a philosophy with which I did not quite agree. That disturbed me. And I was left floating out at sea all by myself. I didn't like it one bit. And I began to fear the worst. I also felt a foreboding of what might lie ahead for the field, because there were changes coming—fast! A cutthroat environment was emerging with profit being its only goal. (See transcript of article written by me in 1999 about the future of work/life on page 83)

I have to interject some personal history at this point in my narrative. My marriage was falling apart. In the summer of 1999, my husband and I separated, and by April of 2000, after twenty-seven years of marriage, we were divorced. That is a very long story, but it certainly added to my sense of discomfort and failure. I was not in a happy place, and I needed a change. I clearly remember having dinner with Elanna Yallow in Boston one evening, when she came to check in on how things were going with me. I was suffering from a head cold and felt pretty miserable, as I disclosed to her that I was going through a divorce. She must have thought that I was a complete mess! I wasn't really. Once a decision was made, I was fine with moving forward, and that's exactly what I did. I had dealt with the pain and the difficulty within my marriage long before that, so I was quite ready to look ahead to the future and new challenges. It took me a little while longer, but later that year, I gave my notice to Knowledge Beginnings and left the company. It was abrupt. I didn't even consider the alternatives. I just knew that I needed a change.

I moved into a luxury apartment in Boston, and I continued with my consulting for about a year, but then I decided to make a complete turnaround. I bought an antique business on Martha's Vineyard and moved to my vacation home full time.

There is much more to tell about this transition, and you can read about it in my book *Reunited: When the Past Becomes a Present.*

My Largest Clients

The Howard Johnson Company

Hill Holiday Connors Cosmopulos

Bronner Slosberg Humphrey

New England Baptist Hospital

Dunkin' Donuts

Owens Corning

Harvard University

Burger King

The State of North Carolina's Smart Start Program

Ryder Corporation

Hasbro, Inc.

UAW (United Auto Workers) Chrysler

UMASS Medical Center

ORGANIZATIONS

5

The Alliance and AWLP

Simultaneous to everything I have already outlined about my personal journey within the work/life industry, I was engaged in working side-by-side with my colleagues and other pioneers of the field to form alliances to advance the message and create a movement. A large percentage of my time during those twenty years (1981 to 2001) was spent on that volunteer effort.

Thus, in my mind, I have saved the best for last. The best—in terms of what I am most proud—and that is the birth and development of The National Work Family Alliance and The Alliance of Work/Life Professionals. I have mentioned several times that I enjoy networking and bringing people together. Essentially, I believe the major impact and contribution I made to the development of the work/life field was my ability to do just that. From my early days of founding and helping to grow The New England Employer-Supported Child Care Network, I continued to join forces with others and advocate for working together to get our message out there to develop awareness on the part of corporate executives.

Frankly, achieving that was a bit of a struggle, too. It seemed like some of the biggest players in the field were not on board when it came to collaboration. I remember distinctly walking away from a meeting at a colleague's hotel room while at the NAEYC annual conference in Atlanta way back in the early 80s, as we were all just getting started. Stephanie Fanjul and I attended the meeting together in hopes that some of the newly formed groups/companies would form an association. Sandy Burud attended that meeting, too, but her reaction was, "Why would I want to share my information and work with others?" Stephanie and I were dumbfounded that Sandy thought that it wasn't a very good idea. Sandy had been one of my original heroes and mentors, and it would have been nice to have her support and assistance while growing our alliance, but she, instead, waited until AWLP was a proven commodity and she was able to reap the benefits of all of our work. It wasn't until years later when our alliances and associations became viable, strong, and important elements within the field that Sandy became involved, even serving as President of AWLP—long after I was out of the picture. There were others who were also late to jump on the band wagon.

ACCCI—The Association of Child Care Consultants International

The result of that meeting in Atlanta that I referenced earlier was the creation of the ACCCI—The Association of Child Care Consultants International. Stephanie Fanjul served as a keynote speaker at the organization's first conference. The Board of that group . . . Mary Ellen Gornick, Madeleine Fried, Stephanie

Fanjul, Clark Adams, Karen Woodford, Roger Neugebauer and me . . . met at my Martha's Vineyard house to discuss our goals and plans for the future. Several other meetings at my home followed as the years progressed.

Final meeting of the ACCCI Board, 1994(?) at
Ann Vincola's house, West Tisbury, MA.
1st row: Roger Neugebauer, Madeline Fried,
Stephanie Fanjul, Ann Vincola.
2nd row: Angela Heath, Mary Ellen Gornick,
(Administrative Assistant from Madeline Fried's
office), Clark Adams, Karen Woodford.

ACCCI continued to exist and to meet separately at the various conferences available to us, especially the NAEYC conference. There is no question that our association helped move the needle forward and give those of us who were like-minded a platform from which to build our expertise and market our services. Of course, the focus for the group was on child care.

The National Work Family Alliance

Then in the early 90s a new group appeared on the scene.

In 1989 I was contacted by a young woman who was completing her graduate research project on work and the family at the University of Michigan in Ann Arbor. That young woman was Kathy Cramer. Kathy came to meet with me at my office on Congress Street in Boston. I liked Kathy a lot. And I was thrilled about her idea—convening a group of leaders in the work/family arena to move the agenda forward. As Kathy began her quest, she soon realized that there were many groups and individuals involved with the same work all over the country, but they didn't know one another. She wanted to change that.

Kathy crisscrossed the United States meeting with key individuals to promote her concept. I was all in. And I gave her all the support that I could. It took a few years to get it together, but eventually we formed an Advisory Committee of sixteen leaders in the field and we met in Boston on November 5, 1992. That group ultimately evolved into The National Work Family Alliance Board of Directors.

In early spring of 1993, the new Alliance Board met at my home on Martha's Vineyard to get us moving in a positive and cohesive direction. Subsequent meetings of the board were not only inspirational, but they were also so much fun. We were dizzy and thrilled with what we were achieving, and we were bound and committed to one another to get us there.

That first board meeting at my house on Lamberts Cove Road in West Tisbury, Massachusetts, was remarkable in itself. Eleven women from that original board stayed at my house and the men in the group stayed across the street at my neighbor,

Muriel Fisher's house. With whiteboard and flip boards ready, we worked hard for an entire weekend designing our organization and modifying our purpose, vision, and goals.

That first weekend gathering was an event—no doubt about it. I remember getting rather nervous about the fact that my stove/oven at my house was old, and perhaps I should buy a new one, especially after Tyler Phillips contacted me and informed me that the group would be doing some communal cooking! So, I bought a new stove before anyone arrived.

Tyler provided each of us with index cards with appetizer, entree, and dessert recipes on them that we were to follow to prepare the delectable meal he planned. This was to be a "bonding activity." We each had instructions and a role to play in the preparation. The activity turned out to be entertaining and convivial. And those index cards appeared at each and every subsequent board meeting which followed at locations around the country—with a new menu! Although he was teased incessantly about his obsessive attention to detail, we laughed, bonded, and enjoyed some pretty fantastic meals. As Roger Neugebauer stated, "Tyler Phillips' collective cooking extravaganzas are something I'll never forget."

And, least I forget, at every gathering, or dinner, for that matter, the person in charge of the wine . . . was Clark Adams. He was our wine connoisseur, and he always made the right selection or brought along the perfect liquid companion to our delectable meals. Clark also found the best restaurants for us to visit no matter in what city we found ourselves.

During that gathering we planned the inaugural National Work/Family Summit, which was held in Washington, DC, a month later. This was significant because it was the first time that leaders from a huge range of constituencies from all over the country convened to discuss the future of the new emerging field of work and family.

We tried to coordinate that meeting with other national events to make it easier for people to attend. However, a major snowstorm interfered somewhat! Those of us who were traveling from the northeast got to Washington a day late forcing us to delay the opening of the Summit. I vividly remember that trip! I was driving solo, because I intended to continue on to Florida after the summit, meet with a client, and see my son who was a student at The University of Miami. My daughter and a friend were meeting us as well. The snowstorm hit the first day of my trip and I got as far as The Delaware River Bridge when the roads became too treacherous to continue traveling. I had to stop, find a motel for the night, and push on the next day. That in itself wasn't the easiest proposition. But I finally made it. Brad Googins, also traveling from Boston, had a difficult time, too. The travel stories kind of made it even more of an historical event.

The Summit became a symbolic and forceful milestone in our quest for recognition of our mission, but also for our individual significance within the growing field. Remember that all of our work, energy, time, and spirit were on a volunteer basis. Some of us were entrepreneurs with our own company, and we were required to foot the bill for the travel and time ourselves. Others were employed by an agency or institution and were given the blessing from their parent company to spend the time and money necessary. We never could have achieved what we did without the thousands of volunteer hours we put in to make it happen.

The National Work Family Alliance continued to operate as a viable and recognizable organization that promoted advocacy for the work/family agenda amid a cross-section of companies, institutions, labor, academics, providers, and the media. As we continued on our journey, we named Kathy Cramer as Executive Director of the organization, and she served in that capacity in its early days.

We knew that we had started something worthwhile, and we had accomplished something big by creating 'The Alliance.'

The Merger of ACCCI and The National Work Family Alliance

As both organizations continued to grow, we soon realized that the groups sometimes struggled to attract the same membership base, even though the two groups shared the same vision, mission, and goals. It became clear to us that a combined professional organization could provide all members with more—under one roof—so to speak. Clark Adams and I served as board members to both organizations and we were the first to admit that combining forces for a common cause made absolute sense.

The two organizations merged in 1996 and from then on, we were *The Alliance of Work/Life Professionals*. By pooling our resources and talents we became a significant and distinguishable field with our own professional organization. The original Board of Directors included: Clark Adams, Mary Ellen Gornick, Bradley Googins, Susan Ginsberg, Tyler Phillips, Karen Woodford, Roger Neugebauer, Donna Dolan, Madeline Fried, Carey Fleming, Kathy Tama, Susan Seitel, and me, Ann Vincola. Mary Ellen Gornick and Brad Googins were named co-presidents of the newly formed joint organization.

Carey Fleming was chair of the first conference presented after the merger took place in 1996 in Charleston,

South Carolina—"Navigating the Currents of the Changing Workplace." It was a great beginning for the new organization to make its mark.

The Alliance of Work/Life Professionals

And, indeed, we made our mark. Over the next several years The AWLP enjoyed increased recognition and growth in membership that was unparalleled in our industry. And I would like to think that I played an important role in making that happen, since I served as Conference Chair of The AWLP National Conference for two years following the merger of the two organizations. I humbly believe that the success of the conference was the key that catapulted us to new heights.

I never wished to be President of our new professional organization . . . I left that to Mary Ellen Gornick. But I LOVED being conference chair. Together, Mary Ellen and I formed a unique team and we worked very hard to nurture AWLP in those early days. I think we spoke on the phone almost daily. As membership grew, so did attendance at our conference.

The first conference that I chaired was held at the Hotel Del Coronado in San Diego, California, in 1997, and was entitled "Reflections on the Future: New Connections, Bold Directions." It was a huge success with over 600 attendees. When I think back on everything I did during my work/life career, I can honestly say that serving as conference chair was the very best, and I loved everything about it. I loved creating and building an agenda, developing workshops, engaging speakers (both keynote speakers and panelists), designing the brochure (I was a stickler for perfection, and I proofread that thing over and over and over again!), and working with hotel staff to plan menus, room allocations, signage, etc.

I was in my element. And I was good at it. I remember walking around the grounds of the hotel on the day before the conference started, with my clipboard in hand and looking very officious—but happy. Betsy Richards, a fellow consultant at BrownRichards & Associates, stopped me, and she took my picture. I usually don't like having my picture taken, but Betsy insisted. She sent me a blown up black and white of that shot after the conference was over. I held on to that photo for years. I even framed it and hung it at my Vineyard house—something I had never done before and haven't done since. But I liked that photo of me. I think that it reflected my comfort and ease, and, yes, joy, that I felt at the time. Anytime anyone remarked about the photo, I always responded with: "That's when I was at the top of my game!"

There were many high-caliber presentations at the conference—both keynote speakers and in workshops. I was very pleased at the quality and strength of the program and grateful to all who participated. Engaging those participants and securing their commitment to speak was always a highlight of the job for me. There is one individual, however, who made a special lasting impression and impact on me.

The Friday luncheon speaker was Judith Rosener, a diversity consultant and author. I got to know Judy prior to the conference, and I was delighted that she agreed to speak. She wrote a groundbreaking article in 1990 that appeared in the *Harvard Business Review* entitled, "How Women Lead." Judy was bigger than life—funny, bright, and right on the money with her quips and remarks.

Judy and I clicked—big time. She lived in Newport Beach, California, and she invited me to her house to see her orchid collection, after she told me about her wonderful hobby. I never got to visit her home, but I think of Judy often, as I have now become an orchid collector and aficionado at my own home in Sarasota, Florida, almost thirty years later. Ironically, I learned of her passing at age ninety-five, just about the same time that I started writing this book.

The next year the AWLP Conference was held in Miami, Florida, at the Intercontinental Hotel, and I was named conference chair once again. The theme of that conference was "New Dimensions for Work/Life: Launching the 21st Century." For the second time I was charged with pulling off a major event—and, for the second time, I loved every minute of it.

I was pretty familiar with Miami by then since I had two major clients there—Burger King and Ryder Corporation. I made regular trips from Boston to Miami to also visit my son, a student at The University of Miami from 1993 to 1997. Therefore, I was very familiar with downtown, South Beach, Coconut Grove, Coral Gables, and other local attractions, including the best restaurants. It was a fun place for our group to descend upon, and we certainly took advantage of everything Miami had to offer.

There are many memories that stick out for me from that conference, but I feel my biggest accomplishment was to secure Change Management Consultant, Rosabeth Moss Kanter, as one of our keynote speakers. It took a bit of maneuvering and coaxing as I spoke with her office at Goodmeasure, Inc. in Cambridge, Massachusetts, many times before securing her commitment to speak. Rosabeth is the author of over twenty books and is currently the Ernest L. Arbuckle Professor of Business at Harvard

Business School, as well as director and chair of the Harvard University Advanced Leadership Initiative. Her book *The Change Masters,* written in 1983, is her most significant contribution to the field. To me she has been the most influential leader in business and change management during her illustrious career. I was tickled pink that she finally said yes!

And she said yes, partly because she was easily able to get the boat across to her home on Fisher's Island after she completed her speaking obligation at the conference. The boat launch was adjacent to the Intercontinental Hotel. As we stood outside the hotel, saying goodbye, before she got the boat over to the island, I thanked her profusely for joining us at our conference. I will never forget her response to me. I told her that it was such an honor to have someone of her notoriety at our conference, and she said, "Well, don't sell yourself short. What you do is pretty special, too." Wow! I was bowled over.

Another accomplishment of mine during that conference was to get trend forecaster Gerald Celente of *The Trends Journal* as another major speaker. After becoming aware of Gerald Celente and his work, I discovered that he was from Yonkers, New York, (my hometown), and his brother was a classmate of mine at Gorton High School. As an American business consultant and trend forecaster, Gerald has published his journal since 1980 and has been interviewed on numerous television news outlets over the years. His predictions on global economics and geopolitics were of particular interest to us. Gerald and I also realized that we had much in common having grown up in an Italian American family, and we had such fun getting to know one another again and discussing our past. For me, his participation was another highlight of that conference.

Something else that has stuck in my mind from that conference is a note I received from Ellen Galinsky after I sent out my 'thank you' letters to all of our speakers. Ellen wrote to me: "Thank you for all you do for our field." That meant so very much to me.

At those two conferences we initiated the AWLP Work-Life Innovative Excellence Award and then went on to join forces with Boston College Center for Work & Family to introduce the Work-Life Certificate Program. AWLP continued to grow in both membership and in the breadth and depth of its programming, even convening regional network events.

Following the merger, our considerably large board (sixteen members) met on a regular basis once or twice a year. We changed the location from east coast to west coast and in between, so as not to make the travel too difficult for any of us. We eagerly anticipated those gatherings. We were like family. We had fun. And we worked hard to expand and spread our mission.

Several of those gatherings were memorable. One year we met in Santa Fe, New Mexico, and rented a house where most of us stayed. Tyler Phillips' index cards became a big part of that meeting, as did his chef's knives! Any good cook worth his salt always brought his knives along. As Clark Adams remarked to me when recalling that Tyler always traveled with his knives,—"Have knives, will travel!" In fact, several of us, having arrived a day early, were charged with grocery shopping in order to have the requisite ingredients on hand for the sumptuous meal to which we would later imbibe. We had our trusty index cards with the shopping list in hand as we carried out Tyler's instructions. Lots of laughs and good fun. Most of the group went out salsa dancing that first evening, and by all accounts, had a grand old time. I stayed back at the house and was so pleased to have the opportunity of spending the evening in conversation with Brad Googins. It was the first time I had the chance to really get to know him.

Another meeting was held at Brad Googins' summer home on the coast of Maine. We enjoyed spending another glorious weekend at Tyler Phillips' home in Tiburon, California. And Clark Adams hosted a gathering at his home in Vermont. Another meeting, toward the end of my tenure, was held at Jane Ginsberg Kershner's house at Yosemite National Park in California. And, most likely the last board meeting that I attended, before ending my service, was in Seattle, Washington. A few of us stayed on and spent a few days on Orcas Island, one of the San Juan Islands off the coast of Seattle. What a lovely spot.

By 2000 several of the founding Board members of AWLP transitioned off and a new board was elected by the membership. The name of the organization changed to the Alliance for

Dinner on Lopez Island after Seattle Board Meeting, 1999.
Ann Vincola, Sue Storgaard, Carey Fleming, Madeline Fried.

Work-Life Progress with recognition from *Fortune* magazine and The American Business Collaboration. And in 2004 AWLP officially became an affiliate of WorldatWork, the world's leading not-for-profit professional association dedicated to knowledge leadership in compensation, benefits, and total rewards . . . and, now, worklife. Kathie Lingle served as Executive Director from 2004 to 2014.

In 2006 AWLP celebrated its tenth anniversary by holding its annual conference in March at the Hilton in Austin, Texas. WorldatWork published a booklet honoring the founding members of AWLP and providing a look at the organization's growth and history. All of the founding members were interviewed for the booklet with a very nice bio and photo of each of us included. Some of my photos that I have used in this book were also used in the booklet after I provided them to the editors.

Boat ride at Seattle Board Meeting, 1999.
Susan Ginsberg, Fran Riley, John Webb, Donna ?, Ann Vincola,
Alice Campbell, Donna Dolan, Sandy Burud, Kathy Tama.

As the Founding Board Members of AWLP, we knew we had accomplished something great, and the tenth anniversary celebration was testament to that. We were very proud to be in on the ground floor of this dynamic organization—and I was especially proud of the role I played.

And that is where my journey ended. I left the field in 2001 and changed my consulting hat to that of a retail business owner. Even so . . . work/life balance continues to be ever-present on my mind.

Not to be Overlooked

Kathleen Beauchesne

Alice Campbell

Kathleen Christensen

Dean Debnam

Netsy Firestein

Stew Friedman

Bernadette Fusaro

Mary Genkins

Brad Harrington

Patricia Herlihy

Jane Ginsberg Kershner

Marci Koblenz

Marcia Brumit Kropf

Kathie Lingle

Linda Marks

Denise Montana

Toni Riccardi

Linda Roundtree

Celina Pagani-Tousignant

Eddie Trieber

John Webb

[Note: These individuals continued the work started in the 80s by the Pioneers. I also had a special connection with all of them.]

THE FUTURE

6

What Came Next

I have included lots of information and detail here and have done my best to be fair and accurate—as best my memory allows. And I know that I have left out individuals who probably should be included, but it was my intent to focus on those professionals who were closest to me and were part of my growth and development within the field.

I can't think of a better way to end my reflection on what started almost forty years ago than to reprint one of the last articles I wrote in 1999. That article looked toward the future. Here it is.

What's Ahead For Work/Life

February 8, 1999

The work/life field should prepare itself for changes. Ann Vincola, Senior Partner of Corporate Work/Life Consulting and a pioneer in the work/life field, offers her insights into the trends the industry will experience in 1999 and beyond:

The work/life industry will continue to ride the wave of mergers and acquisitions. Acquisitions will continue as companies strive to contain cost and enhance delivery of service.

Employers will become more careful in how they spend their work/life dollars. Employers will continue to stress measurement and return on investment of work/life dollars. But they are becoming more sophisticated and will move beyond focusing solely on measurement issues. They are going to cut certain programs and become increasingly careful in selecting vendors.

Vendors will need to focus on flexibility and responsiveness. As employers become more sophisticated and acceptance and understanding of work/life issues becomes increasingly universal, vendors will no longer assume the role of educators. Instead, they will be focusing on responsiveness and delivery of service—creating programs tailored to clients' specific needs.

Work/life programs will continue to be outsourced. As companies examine and scrutinize their work/life programs and become more calculated in what they are offering, they will look toward outsourcing as a way to manage cost and enhance quality.

The lines between wellness, employee assistance and work/life programs will be blurred. As healthcare costs continue to rise, employers will see the benefit of pulling together all risk prevention programs—wellness, EAP, and work/life under one umbrella.

Businesses will make larger investments in education. On-site child care facilities are evolving into learning centers and employers are paying more attention to schools and educating the youth of America.

Work/life programs will need to be integrated into company intranets. Resource and referral programs will become technology-driven and will be integrated in company intranets.

Multi-generational workplaces will continue to affect work/life strategies. With mature workers, Baby Boomers, Generation Xers, and the now-emerging Generation Y working side-by-side, companies will need to create work/life programs that motivate a workforce that, at times spans 62 years.

Work/life programs will play a more critical role in downsizing efforts. Successful downsizing—and other change efforts—requires that companies focus on the people within the organization. To ease the transition for surviving employees, companies will need to have work/life programs in place before the change occurs.

Companies will offer more spousal benefits. Companies have found that focusing on family members—especially spouses—enhances the success of career changes such as relocation. As a result, there will be more of an emphasis to include spouses in areas such as training and career development.

Work/life will be integrated into a company's global strategy. As global mergers and acquisitions, the use of expatriates, and global relocation continue to rise, companies will need to focus on creating global work/life strategies.

Corporate America will witness a resurgence in employee commitment and loyalty. As employers continue to see the benefit of taking care of their employees, employees will respond with enhanced commitment and loyalty.

Source: *Ann Vincola, Senior Partner, Corporate Work/ Life Consulting, a subsidiary of Knowledge Beginnings, Boston, MA.*

Was I on the money? Did I get it right? Was I prescient as to what was to come? I think I was correct on several points, but we never know what the future will bring, nor how the economy will change, or how the political climate might impact progress. All of that influences how corporate America reacts.

And where are we headed now—today, forty years after we started the ball rolling?

Are we moving forward or going backwards? Is everything, including attention to work/life balance issues, potentially cyclical? Are working mothers leaving the workforce to stay at home with their children?

Is the child care system sufficient? Are corporate leaders requiring employees to go back to the office? Is remote work being reduced now that the pandemic is over? Are hybrid working teams becoming obsolete? And is mental health a bigger issue today than it was so many years ago?

The workplace is changing again, and corporate execs will need to rely on human resource and work/life consultants as they did in the 80s and 90s to help implement programs that make sense to diverse workforces, and to help employees balance their work and personal lives. We were the ones to do it then. Who will do it now?

Thanks for joining me on my memory journey and allowing me to recollect so much of my career path. I was so proud to be part of the growth of a movement.

AFTERWORD

Afterword

A s I completed the text for my book, describing my history
and involvement in the growth of the work/life movement,
I realized that I had two other articles authored by me in 1998
and 2000, respectively, that substantiate all that I have shared
in my book. I believe the content of these articles help make the
case for continued attention to how work/life balance figures in
our lives today. The following two articles stress two concepts:
first, how companies can and must survive in a global economy;
and, secondly, the importance of implementing elder care programs and policies, as we enter the era of an aging workforce.

Taking Your Work/Life Policy Abroad

Craft a work/life policy with a global perspective.
By Ann Vincola

As corporate boundaries extend worldwide, an organization's
scope of work/life programs must expand as well. No longer able
to view work/life issues solely through *American glasses*, companies

must look at work/life issues from a global perspective. Motivating and supporting today's global workforce means addressing the diverse needs and desires of all employees. Companies, therefore, must be cautious to offer benefits that are meaningful and are valued across cultures.

Work/life programs are on the rise.

U.S. businesses are getting serious about helping their employees balance work and family commitments. A 1998 survey by Bethesda, Maryland-based Watson Wyatt Worldwide reports that flex options, job sharing and other scheduling alternatives are moving into the corporate mainstream. Half of all large U. S. companies surveyed, and nearly a third of mid-sized companies, are making nontraditional arrangements commonplace.

Work/life benefits are gaining acceptance largely because companies see the link between high morale and outstanding performance. According to this year's "Best Companies" study by *Fortune* magazine, 73 percent of those that made the inaugural list of "100 Best Places to Work in America" reported much higher than average annual returns on investment.

It's also encouraging that work/life issues are receiving high-level attention from some of the country's largest corporations. Last year more than 70 CEOs gathered in New York City for the first CEO summit on work/family issues. "Our very presence today says something about the new realities of leading a company in the global marketplace," said Paul Allaire, CEO of Xerox based in Stamford, Connecticut.

A global work/life strategy is essential for worldwide success.

As companies continue to embrace work/life strategies, they must be sure to approach the strategies from a global perspective. Today, more than 100,000 U.S. firms are engaged in some type of global venture with a combined value of more than $1 trillion. One of every five American workers is employed at a company with a global presence, and the number is increasing daily. In fact, U.S. multinational companies employ almost seven million people outside the United States.

To offer benefits and policies that are meaningful to a global workforce, companies must assess work/life issues within the context of their employees' social, cultural, and country backgrounds. Understanding the distinction between U.S. and European views of work/family issues, for example, will help American companies to create valuable work/life strategies for their European employees.

As stated in a recent report by The Center for Work & Family at Boston College, in European countries "work and family issues tend to be regarded as socio-political as well as economic concerns...It's widely expected that all social partners—including workplaces, governments, and trade unions—should be involved in addressing work and family issues. Work and family priorities are not regarded as being primarily a corporate concern."

In the United States, these issues generally are seen as a combination of professional matters and family concerns. Economic and social concerns typically are considered separately. In Europe, however, work and family issues are closely connected, and economic and social progress is seen as inextricably linked. As a result, European social legislation provides for such basic, family-friendly benefits as national health care, although employers are increasingly looked to for additional family-friendly policies and practices.

European countries provide basic work/family benefits.

Many European countries provide significant baseline support for employees. Corporations doing business in Europe should look at the benefits already provided by individual countries when developing work and family programs there. The following is a look at some work/life issues and how they're handled in different European countries:

1. Child Care:

Benefits often are addressed at the workplace. In countries such as the Netherlands, the United Kingdom and Portugal, employer-based child care and child care allowances are becoming common. In other countries, such as Sweden, universal child care is publicly provided.

2. Maternity/parental leave rights:

Under national health services, basic benefits are provided by all European governments. Very generous attitudes exist toward maternity leaves and, in some countries, paternity leaves, parental leaves and leaves to care for sick family members. For instance, employees in Sweden enjoy 38 weeks of paid parental leave at 90 percent of their pay.

3. Health care:

Europe has a national health service program that provides health insurance and dependent health care, significantly reducing the need for employers to provide this benefit.

4. Telecommuting:

Because of advances in telecommunications and computer technology, there has been an increase in telecommuting in Europe, most notably in the United Kingdom and the Netherlands.

5. Career breaks:

Structured like a sabbatical, career breaks are offered by companies in France, Germany, and Belgium and usually are used for child care or schooling.

6. Alternative work options:

European companies have offered flextime for many years. Use of part-time and job-sharing options has increased in recent years, particularly in the United Kingdom, Germany, and France.

While many European countries provide employees with basic benefits, there is recognition that more assistance from employers is needed to help families meet their professional and personal responsibilities. The expectation is growing that companies will assume a greater role in helping employees to balance their work and family lives through employer-sponsored benefits and programs.

As in numerous European countries, many Asian governments and social institutions value the family as an essential institution and are committed to its well-being. For example, in Singapore sustaining traditional values and preserving family strength are considered intangible factors in the success of East Asian economies. In support of a family-friendly workplace, government-sponsored benefits offered to employees include:

- Eight weeks paid maternity leave

- Four years unpaid maternity leave

- Four years unpaid child care leave for parents with sick children

- Eldercare

- Child care subsidies

- Family resource centers

"Our institutions and basic policies are in place to sustain high economic growth. But if we lose our traditional values, our family strength and cohesion, we will lose our vibrancy—and decline," states Goh Chol Tong, Singapore's Prime Minister.

Connect your policy to company objectives.

Global competition requires that American corporations develop a work/life strategy that supports their overall business objectives. This approach becomes even more critical when considering the influx of workforce issues that have emerged in recent years, such as gender equity, diversity, wellness, health, and stress management. Add to this mix the issues concerning expatriates, and it becomes obvious that a strategic approach to work/life issues is essential

One company that has been successful in addressing the variety of work/life issues of its global workforce is SC Johnson

Wax, located in Racine, Wisconsin. A manufacturer of household cleaning, personal care, and insect control products with more than 12,000 employees and 100 expatriates, the company has developed a program that provides compensation and benefits to globally transferred employees. Covered under a uniform transfer policy, the program links compensation and benefits to an employee's home country.

In addition to making it relatively easy to transfer employees around the work, the program recognizes the complexity of the social and national health and benefit programs provided by many countries. Under a uniform policy, work/life issues can be easily addressed assuring that the employee's work/life needs are met.

Indianapolis-based Eli Lilly also recognizes that there are many unique work/life issues involved when transferring families in and out of the United States. "We learned a few years ago how important it is to place a lot of focus on the family's needs. It's kind of like a domino effect. If the children aren't happy, the spouse isn't going to be happy, the employee isn't going to be happy, and the company isn't going to be happy. It can all tumble down on you," says Samuel L. Pearson, Eli Lilly's International Relocation Coordinator.

Realizing that schooling is a critical issue and seeking to make the transition easier for inpatriates, the Indiana-based producer of human health and agricultural products helped found the International School of Indiana. Serving children in pre-K through grade three, the school grew from38 students to 81 in its first two years. "With the help of other multinational companies, we expect to expand the school to a complete elementary school," says Pearson.

Companies with meaningful programs are rewarded by greater employee commitment.

Studies confirm that people today want more balance between their work and family lives and companies would be wise to adapt. Additional reports show that employees who use work/family programs receive the highest job performance ratings and have the highest commitment to the company. In a business world where corporations are downsizing, merging, and restructuring, a motivated and loyal workforce will be a company's greatest asset.

"Individual energy and creativity are unleased when changes in work practices benefit employees' personal lives," said Xerox's Allaire. "The best business strategy recognizes that greater employee satisfaction means greater productivity and, in turn, better business results."

The changing needs of today's workforce have created unprecedented demands for flexible and diverse programs and policies. While companies are realizing the benefits of implementing a work/life strategy, it is essential that they do so from a global perspective. As. U.S. companies continue to expand operations across borders, the ability to maintain a productive and motivated workforce is critical to success.

Companies that incorporate the global perspective into their work/life strategy will have a competitive advantage in today's global market. For American corporations, the difference between success and failure may be how well they learn to manage their global workforce.

Ann Vincola is Senior Vice President of Work/Life Benefits, heading its consulting division and Boston office. (July, 1998)

Elder Care – What Firms Can Do To Help

Due to demographics there is an increase in the number of
workers caring for elderly relatives.
By Ann Vincola

Working caregivers now comprise a large part of the workforce.
Due to simple demographics, many employees—surveys put the
number at 10 percent or higher—find themselves having to care
for aging parents or relatives, often in addition to caring for their
own children. Besides "working caregivers," who provide primary
care, there is another group of workers who provide long-distance
care to parents or relatives with disabilities. Obviously, the toll
this kind of stress takes on the employee is enormous.

Costs

In addition, there are costs to the company, including absenteeism,
workday interruptions, recruitment costs (to replace employees
who quit) and decreased productivity in general.

While elder care needs are not new, as it becomes more
prevalent, the issue is being pushed to the forefront. The greatest
increase in the numbers of elderly in North America is expected
between the years 2010 and 2030, when the baby boom generation turns 65. The typical caregiver is a 46-year-old employed
woman who spends approximately 18 hours pr week caring for
her mother. The average duration of caregiving is 4.5 years, but
that figure is likely to increase as medical advances prolog life.

A Hewitt Associates survey of work and family benefit plans
of Fortune 500 companies found that in 1996, nearly one-third

of the employers offered elder care programs. This represents an increase of 17 per cent over 1991. Most of the companies—79 percent—offered resource and referral programs. Long-term care insurance was offered by 25 percent of the employers with elder care programs, up from 5 percent in 1991.

A 1997 study in the U.S. found that elder care benefits are not offered as often the public sector, with only seven percent of responding agencies indicating that they offer elder care assistance. Whatever the work/life benefits available, supervisors' attitudes and behavior can make or break the usefulness of the program. While a benefit may exist on paper, managers can send mixed signals when the employees try to use the benefit.

How organizations can help.

Since elder care is a problem likely to affect every company sooner or later, the time to establish resources is now. The first step is to conduct a needs survey. A needs analysis can help assess the scope of your firm's employee elder care concerns.

After reviewing data from an employee survey, you can build a program. Here are some elements to consider:

- **Resource and referral**:
  Resource and referral services for elder care help familiarize employees with the available array of services for the elderly, including medical, custodial, legal, and counseling services. You also can provide information about elder care through seminars, support groups, handbooks, hotlines, and your EAP.

Resource and referral services are starting to gain in popularity in the U.S. A recent study found that 23 percent of the companies surveyed offered these services, and an additional five percent are considering it.

- **Subsidies**:
  Your company can offer reimbursement or direct subsidies to employees for costs for visiting nurses or costs associated with hiring a caregiver or respite care.

- **Support Groups**:
  These are often available through hospitals, nursing homes, social service agencies and health councils. America Online even offers an online caregiver support chat group.

- **Employee Assistance Programs**:
  In one study, among respondents using EAPs, the heaviest users were employees with both elder care and child care responsibilities. EAPs serve in a variety of roles to co-ordinate and assist in developing and procuring elder care services.

- **Caregiver fairs**:
  Caregiver fairs are becoming popular. They are held through public groups or in conjunction with organizations and private corporations. They are usually four hours long and held in a strategic location, such as a cafeteria or lobby. They include creative promotional activities, elder care service vendors who run exhibits, and mini-tip sessions in conjunction with the fair to address a variety of elder care issues.

- **Counseling**:

  The University of California at Berkeley has a pilot program under which an on-site, licensed clinical social worker provides assessment and counseling to faculty and staff on elder care and adult dependent care issues.

- **Long-term care insurance**:

  This helps employees pay for long-term care for themselves or dependent children, spouses, or parents.

- **Adult day care**:

  Employers can support local, adult day care centers with financial or in-kind contributions. These facilities offer adult day programs for the elderly; adult day programs are also available in hospitals and other care facilities.

- **Emergency care**:

  The purpose of emergency care is to assure that assistance will be available when regular arrangements are not, or when other circumstances dictate a short-term need. For example, a consortium of seven businesses, primarily law firms, began a program at no cost to employees for emergency in-home child and elder care. Administered by Caregivers on Call, the service is available 24-hours-a-day, seven-days-a-week, year-round, when employee's usual child or elder care arrangements fall through.

- **Elder care pager programs**:

  Some companies have elder care pager programs in which they provide a free pager to employees with needs related to elder care.

- **Flexible spending accounts**:
  In dependent care assistance programs or flexible spending accounts in the U.S., the employer and employee agree to reduce the employee's income by a certain amount to be placed in a dependent care assistance fund for the employee. Employee benefit surveys suggest that only a small percentage of employees use such accounts, although some companies subsidize employee contributions to the accounts.

- **Flextime**:
  Arrangements such as telecommuting, compressed work weeks, job sharing, part-time employment, flextime, and bi-weekly work arrangements let staff adapt their schedules to the needs of their families.

Companies are instituting some or all of these options to assure that employees can successfully manage the needs and demands of their family responsibilities and create a better work/life balance for them. Elder care issues continue to pose unique problems for many within today's workforce, and employees are genuinely grateful for any assistance that their company may provide.

Ann Vincola is Senior Partner of Corporate Work/Life Consulting, a subsidiary of Knowledge Beginnings. (June, 2000)

This article was particularly interesting to me, now in 2023, as we have already reached the time when the baby boom population is over 65 and attention is clearly on an aging population.

THE GROWTH OF THE WORK/LIFE MOVEMENT
IN CORPORATE AMERICA

Even more signifantly, we have come through a pandemic, in which many elders' lives were lost. Additionally, as I have turned 80, I hope that the time when I personally will require care is still years from now!

Today, more than ever, work/life programs and policies should be part of a comprehensive employee benefits strategy for all companies.

Bibliography

Burud, Sandra, and Marie Tumolo, *Leveraging the New Human Capital*, October, 2004.

Burud, Sandra, *Employer Supported Child Care*, March, 1984.

Evans, E. Belle, *Designing a Day Care Center: How to Select, Design, and Develop a Day Care Center*, January, 1974.

Evans, E. Belle, Day Care: *How to Plan, Develop, and Operate a Day Care Center*, January, 1971.

Evans, E. Belle, and George E. Saia, *Day Care for Infants: The Case for Infant Day Care and a Practical Guide*, January, 1972.

Kanter, Rosabeth Moss, *The Change Masters: Corporate Entrepreneurs at Work*, 1983.

Kanter, Rosabeth Moss, *Men and Women of the Corporation*, August, 2008.

Kanter, Rosabeth Moss, *Work and Family in the United States: A Critical Review and Agenda for Research and Policy (Social Science Frontiers)*, November, 1977.

Galinsky, Ellen, *Mind in the Making*, April, 2010.

Galinsky, Ellen, *The Six Stages of Parenthood*, January, 1987.

Galinsky, Ellen, *Ask the Children: What America's Children Really Think About Working Parents*, September, 1999.

Thomas Jr., R. Roosevelt, *Beyond Race and Gender: Unleashing the Power of Your Total Workforce by Managing Diversity*, October, 1992.

Thomas Jr., R. Roosevelt, *World Class Diversity Management: A Strategic Approach*, August, 2010.

Thomas Jr. R. Roosevelt, *Building a House for Diversity: A Fable About a Giraffe & an Elephant Offers New Strategies for Today's Workforce*, June, 1999.

In Memoriam

Rick Beinecke

Juliet Brudney

Patricia Cronin

Susan Ginsberg

Dave Gleason

Gwen Morgan

Judith Rossener

R. Roosevelt Thomas Jr.

Faith Wohl

About the Author

After an extensive career as an educator, consultant, and business owner, Ann Vincola Votta is now concentrating on memoir and travel writing, along with her husband (also an author) through their publishing company, AV  Publishing LLC, Sarasota, Florida.

Her background includes fifteen years as a teacher, consultant, and Professor of Early Childhood Education; twenty years as a nationally recognized human resource and work/life consultant; and ten years in retail as owner of an antiques and interiors business on Martha's Vineyard.

She holds a B.A. degree in English from SUNY Cortland, Cortland, New York, and an M.ED. in Administration from Lesley University, Cambridge, Massachusetts.

Made in the USA
Columbia, SC
13 October 2023

24432832R00074